NUAL '95

Get Giggs!

RYAN GIGGS is the most exciting talent in British football. The Manchester United and Wales winger is also the ultimate nightmare for his Premiership opponents. So just how do you keep him quiet? That's the question we put to eight top class defenders who all agreed...he's almost unstoppable!

Like Ian Wright

Lee Dixon - (Arsenal)

RYAN GIGGS has the world at his feet because he's got everything a manager wants - speed, skill, enthusiam - and he scores goals.

He can be your worst nightmare if you let him run at you. You must mark him tight and try to stop him getting the ball - then you have a chance.

Some defenders try to intimidate him but I've never seen him flinch from a challenge. He's quite strong for a smallish lad and is bound to get stronger as he fills out.

I haven't seen a weakness in him yet. He's like Ian Wright - you can't relax against him for a second.

Unbelievable

Mark Bowen (Norwich)

I'M lucky to see Ryan every month or so with the Welsh squad and he gets better every time I see him. He's getting more mature as a

Continued overleaf

person and as a player, which is great for United and for Wales.

Some of the things he does on the training ground are unbelievable. It takes my breath away just watching his skills. I'd settle for half his ability, yet he's not satisfied with what he's got and is always working to improve himself.

He's a very level-headed lad. And because he's surrounded by stars at Old Trafford, he's not at all big-headed. But he's not as silent as most people seem to think. I just hope English football can hold on to him.

Quicker than Baggio

Shaun Teale - (Aston Villa)

YOU normally expect Giggs to come at you down the wings, but he's so versatile that United played him down the middle against us and he never gave us a minute's rest.

He might not look like Charles Atlas, but he's got remarkable body strength and fabulous balance which makes him very difficult to knock off the ball.

It's great for British football that he's playing regular international football. He's the sort of player we need to restore our reputation in the world game.

He's already a world beater and the only player I can compare him to is Italy's Roberto Baggio - except that Giggs looks quicker.

Defender's nightmare

Steve Clarke (Chelsea)

GIGGS is an exceptional player and so level headed. There are some excellent players around at the moment, but only one Ryan Giggs.

He comes at you with pace and represents a defender's nightmare when he is in full flight.

You can't plan to exploit his weaknesses because he doesn't seem to have any. All you can do is make sure you are at your best and hope that is good enough.

I admire him not just for his attacking ability, but his all-round contribution too. He doesn't stand around waiting for the ball and is very good at getting back to help out the midfield and defence.

Out of this world

Brian Borrows (Coventry)

THE only other player in Britain who comes even close to Giggs is our own Peter Ndlovu, but he doesn't have the luxury of ten world class players around him.

When United wiped the floor with us at Old Trafford the other year, Giggs was out of this world. And because he kept popping up all over the place, we were never quite sure who was supposed to be marking him.

Every full-back in the Premiership knows when they're due to face United because a game against Giggs is something really special. An exciting prospect? No, more like your biggest challenge of the season.

I prefer Ince

John Pemberton (Leeds)

THE first requirement for anyone playing against Giggs is pace. If you haven't got that you haven't got a prayer against him. He'll murder you.

He's got so many tricks up his sleeve that it's impossible to pin him down for 90 minutes. The first time I played against Giggs, I gave him a good early dig and went to pick him up and he just shrugged me off. I learned then that he can't be intimidated.

But I'd still have Paul Ince in my team ahead of Giggs. Ryan can turn a game with one bit of magic, but there are times when you want a solid, professional performance and he'll give the ball away trying a trick.

Hard to mark

Dean Austin (Tottenham)

I CAN'T think of anyone who has come on to the scene and taken people's breath away the way Ryan Giggs has. He's got exceptional pace, great skill and a bit of everything else.

He' very hard to mark because he's so versatile. He can beat you any way he likes and a lot of defenders don't really know what to do against him. Even those who give him a whack to let him know that they are there find that he can ride tackles superbly.

He's got so many tricks up his sleeve it's untrue. He obviously works hard on them, and will try things in matches that other players wouldn't even dare.

Under pressure

Tim Breacker (West Ham)

MOST wingers are either tricky with pace or more controlled and better passers. Giggs is the only winger I know with speed of foot and speed of thought, skill, touch and the intelligence to know when to knock it off and when to take you on.

There's an awful lot of pressure on him but he's been handled magnificently by Alex Ferguson and is already one of the best players in the world. And he can only get better.

But because United have so many great players, you can't concentrate all your efforts on Giggs. You have to work out a way to keep them all quiet.

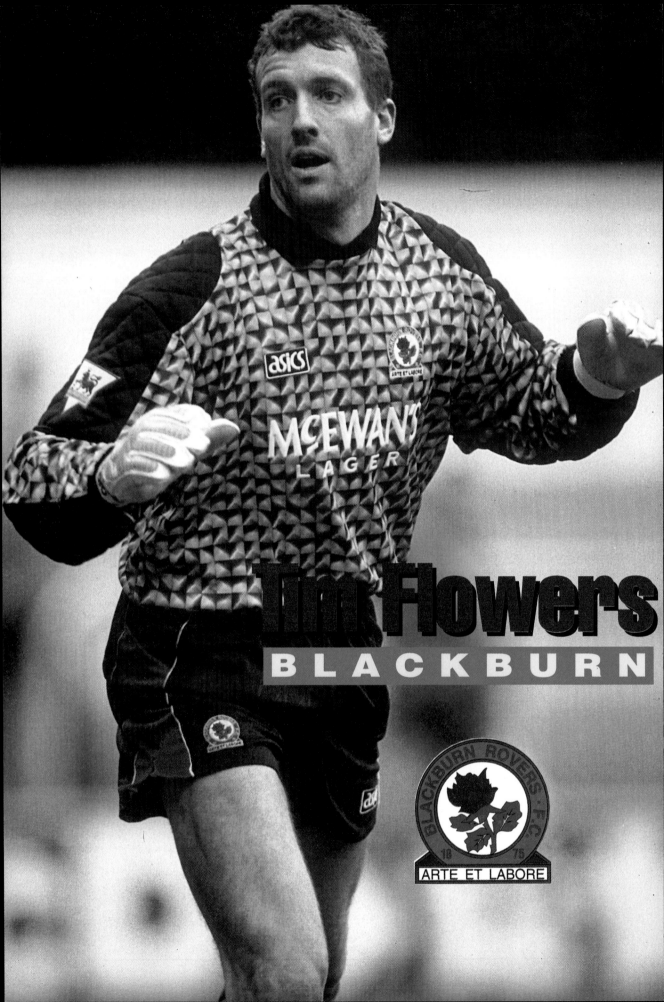

Tim Flowers

BLACKBURN

Paul
Walsh
Man. City

me AL

Ever brought anything you thought was a bit pricey, only to look back and think what a fantastic bargain it actually was?

That's exactly what Kenny Dalglish must be doing right now. The Blackburn Rovers boss smashed the British transfer record in 1992 when he splashed out £3.3m to land England

Alan Shearer is the youngest player ever to score a First Division hat-trick. He was 17 when he struck a triumphant triple against Arsenal

and Southampton hitman Alan Shearer.

Now, only two years later, rumours are rampant that Italian giants Sampdoria have offered £10m for the player they rate as the most complete striker in Europe, ahead of the likes of Van Basten and Bergkamp.

It's very unlikely though that the 23-year-old Geordie goal ace will be leaving Ewood Park as he is still under contract to Rovers for another three years.

Dalglish couldn't, in his wildest dreams, have imagined just

how Shearer's career would take off having joined his band of merry men.

But the England striker had to overcome potential disaster before he became a sensation at Rovers.

A Gazza-style knee ligament injury put his career on hold, and many even dismissed the England star as finished.

"I never listened when people said I should quit," he says.

"I never doubted that I'd come back 100 per cent fit. It took longer than I expected but just as the surgeon said it would be, my knee is stronger than ever."

And to illustrate the point the irrepressible Geordie bounced back with 31 goals last season as Rovers pushed Manchester United all the way in the title race and qualified for Europe for the first time in their history.

Now super Al is set to lead England's strikeforce into the 1996 European Championship.

Yes, that £3.3 million has certainly proved money well spent.

They came from nowhere

BY DAVID MILES

WHEN David Platt was appointed his country's skipper by Terry Venables it completed one of the most amazing turnarounds in football history.

For the 28-year-old Lancashire lad looked to be bombing out of football when Manchester United released him ten years ago. Now he lives in a castle in Italy, owns a restaurant in Wolverhampton and is captain of England.

Platt has Dario Gradi (right) to thank for his transition from soccer's death row to his place on millionaires' row. It was the Crewe boss who rescued him from his Old Trafford obscurity, a feat Gradi has repeated many times since.

England internationals Rob Jones (right) and Geoff Thomas were both given a helping hand by Gradi as they looked to build a career in the big time.

Jones was catapulted into the big league when he walked straight into the Liverpool first team from Gresty Road. Within a of months he played for England against France at Wembley (below).

England strikers Les Ferdinand and Ian Wright have both been plucked from obscurity to star in

John Barnes was discovered playing Sunday League parks football

the Premiership and for their country.

Wright was picked up by Steve Coppell at Crystal Palace from non-League Greenwich Borough and the rest, as they say, is history.

Ian used to laugh off suggestions that one day he would be in the big-money league. The man who is now one of the most feared strikers in Europe admits: "At Palace in the early days I was told I'd be worth £800,000 and I couldn't stop laughing."

Ferdy has taken more time to develop as one of the star strikers in England. The 27-year-old joined QPR from Hayes, but he left London for a spell in Turkey before coming back to fire himself into the national side.

The list of stars who have had a lucky break in getting to the top is endless, but one of the strangest is probably the story of John Barnes.

The Jamaican-born winger eluded the scouts as a teenager only for a Watford fan to recommend him to the Vicarage Road club after seeing him in action for Sudbury Court in Sunday parks football.

But it's nothing new for players to start at the lowest levels of the game and graduate to take some of the games top honours.

Kevin Keegan and Ray Clemence both served apprenticeships at Scunthorpe before making it big at Liverpool and becoming two of English football's greatest names.

With the Premiership's top clubs having contacts all over the world, players are being unearthed from the most unlikely places.

Coventry City discovered a jewel when they picked up Peter Ndlovu from Highlands in Zimbabwe and Millwall's giant keeper Kasey Keller has been a revelation since he went straight into the Lions Den from Portland University.

With the amount of rough diamonds that have turned into finely cut gems over the past few years you could pick a dream team to rival the best out of these finds alone.

The players are all in the £1 million-plus bracket and players of the calibre of Geoff Thomas, Mike Marsh and Neville Southall have been left out.

Les Ferdinand - from Hayes to England

Plucked from Obscurity XI:

Coton (Tamworth);

Jones (Crewe), **Parker** (Fulham), **Peacock** (Hereford), **Pearce** (Wealdstone);

Waddle (Tow Law), **Platt** (Crewe) (capt), **Barnes** (Sudbury Court), **Sharpe** (Torquay);

Ferdinand (Hayes), **Wright** (Greenwich Borough).

Player	Present Club	First Club
Tony Coton	Manchester City	Tamworth
Rob Jones	Liverpool	Crewe
Paul Parker	Manchester United	Fulham
Darren Peacock	QPR	Hereford
Stuart Pearce	Nottingham Forest	Wealdstone
Chris Waddle	Sheffield Wednesday	Tow Law
David Platt (Capt)	Sampdoria	Crewe
John Barnes	Liverpool	Sudbury Court
Lee Sharpe	Manchester United	Torquay
Les Ferdinand	QPR	Hayes
Ian Wright	Arsenal	Greenwich Borough

A Substitute

BU

Meet the men who have more problems with splinters than strikers

Sitting on a freezing cold subs bench for hours on end is hardly much of a life for a footballer.

And for some it required drastic action. Oldham even put in an electrically heated bench at their Boundary Park home.

So even though England's Under-21 'keeper Paul Gerrard lost his place in October last season at least he knew his backside would still be warm by the end of the 90 minutes.

Not so fortunate was the veteran Republic of Ireland keeper Gerry Peyton who was West Ham's No 2 to big Ludo Miklosko last season.

He decided that the chilly afternoons sitting on the Upon Park }sidelines were too much and he jetted off to the Land of the Rising Sun to start a new career alongside Gary Lineker in Japan's J-League.

But Peyton is an exception to the rule. For most reserve goalies it is a question of waiting your turn until the No.1 'keeper gets injured or sent-off.

But when the man between the posts is forced to come off, the reserve must be ready

Norwich's reserve 'keeper Scott Howie watches the action

...ready for action

and able for action in seconds.

Norwich bought the Scotland Under-21 'keeper Scott Howie from Clyde last summer, but he had to be very patient before getting his chance to replace Bryan Gunn.

Last season at Carrow Road, Steve McManaman was in on goal and had his shot handled outside the box by Gunn and was shown the red card with just two

keepers get m Deal

minutes left.

Howie came off the bench and straightaway had to face a thunderbolt free-kick from Liverpool hardman Julian Dicks.

But the Norwich youngster managed to scramble the ball away to save a point for The Canaries.

And after that performance no-one can disagree with Howie when he says: "Being a sub isn't easy. There's a lot more to it than people think.

"It is extremely important to keep your concentration because, as I found out, you can be

David Seaman gets the red card against West Ham - call for the sub!

...and in action

called into the action at any moment."

Chelsea 'keeper Kevin Hitchcock also makes sure he is properly prepared for every game.

He says: "It is obviously frustrating not being in the first-team but I'm a professional and I prepare for every game as if I was playing. But I must admit I hate watching."

And the Blues Russian import Dmitri Kharine can be grateful that he has 'Hitch' for company.

"Dmitri and I spend a lot of time together and I help him with his English.

Believe me, he asks a lot of questions," says Hitchcock.

Howie reveals that he cannot afford to take his eyes off the game for a minute.

He says: "I follow the game as closely as if I was playing. I keep my eye on the ball, and work out what I would have done in situations that arise on the pitch."

And he will then chat to the No. 1 Bryan Gunn over the half-time cup of tea. "Sometimes I might see something in the game and mention it to Bryan at the break and try and help him. But normally he has already seen it himself," says Howie.

Not surprisingly, after his heroics, against Liverpool, Howie is a fan of the rule which allows 'keepers to be replaced during a game.

He says: "If a 'keeper is injured or sent-off and there is no-one to take over it can ruin a match."

A man who would definitely agree is Arsenal's Alan Miller. He was given his chance just seven minutes from time against West Ham last season after David Seaman had dramatically been ordered off.

The professional foul rule has increased the chances of a sub 'keeper being called upon.

Spare a thought for Millwall's Carl Emberson who had never played League football before he was called into play an Anglo-Italian Cup tie last season. His dream debut turned into a nightmare when he was sent-off after just 20 minutes.

Even worse was the experience of Crewe's Mark Smith who was dismissed after an astonishing 19 seconds in a Third Division game last season..

So next time you're at a game, spare a thought for the sub 'keeper who is facing the splinters rather than the strikers!

Da

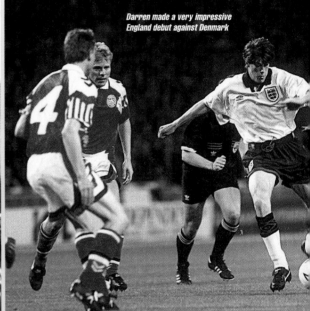

Darren made a very impressive
England debut against Denmark

zza
Darren's the new Gazza

SPURS have always been in the entertainment as well as the trophy business.

The White Hart Lane audience have enjoyed watching stars like Hoddle, Waddle, Ardiles and Gascoigne down the years. And now they are acclaiming current top of the bill act - dazzling Darren Anderton.

Anderton's flicks and tricks are a major feature of Saturday afternoons at the Lane. His ability to cross the ball from virtually any angle is unsurpassed in the country and has replaced Gazza as the new hero of the Spurs fans..

So it's no wonder the doubters who questioned Tottenham's sanity in signing a 20-year-old for £1.7 million have been silenced.

"Spurs are my kind of football club," says Anderton, who has steadily grown in confidence during his two years at White Hart Lane.

"They stand for playing in the right way. And the list of stars they have had here is incredible."

When Anderton signed from Portsmouth, he was given the nickname 'Dazza' - as fans saw him as the replacement for departing 'Gazza'. But the more natural comparison would be with Chris Waddle.

Like Waddle, Anderton runs around the field looking tired and only half-interested. But appearances can be deceptive. Suddenly he will stand up straight, produce an electrifying burst of pace and either lose his marker or send in a devastating cross.

Like Waddle, Anderton also struggled to make an impact in the early days in his attempt to take over the mantle of chief entertainer.

"It was difficult. Everything I tried seemed to go wrong. It seems like a bad memory now and a lot of credit for getting through it must lie with Terry Venables," he says.

"He paid a lot of money for me but tried to take the pressure off. He told me to relax and work hard, and things would work out.

"Terry gave me confidence because he is such a good judge of footballers. He bought myself and Gazza as 20-year-olds and we've all seen what Gazza can do. If I can become half the player he is, I'll be very happy."

Gazza, Hoddle and Waddle were not only White Lane stars but graced the World Cup stage for England.

And Anderton is following that path as well, enjoying his first taste of the international limelight when Venables - now England boss - picked him for the friendly international against Denmark in March.

Anderton proved Wembley's biggest star, tormenting the Danish defence and being denied a debut goal only by a clearance off the line by Marc Rieper.

England won the game 1-0 and has given Anderton the motivation to be a permanent part of the international set-up.

"The whole atmosphere at Wembley was brilliant," he says. "There was a full house and there was a lump in my throat when I walked out the tunnel before kick-off. It was a dream come true, something I had wanted all my life.

"I was terribly nervous before the game started but got an early touch which helped my confidence. By the end I was enjoying it so much, I didn't want the referee to blow the whistle for full-time!"

Anderton, the ungainly schoolboy cross country runner, has become Anderton the pedigree footballer.

Venables, who has seen countless Spurs stars in his time at White Hart Lane as player manager and Chief Executive thinks the fresh-faced 22-year-old has what it takes to rank alongside the very best.

He says: "He has that ability to pick out the right pass very early. He gets half a yard on his man and puts in the early cross which is invaluable to striker. He doesn't check back unnecessarily. His England debut was of the highest order.

"He can play wide, he can tuck in, he can play up front or handle a roving commission. And he is strong enough to be no pushover in the tackle."

With a CV like that, no wonder Anderton is being welcomed into the exclusive club of superstars who have lit up White Hart Lane.

Peter Ndlovu *is better than*

THAT's the verdict of former Coventry manager Bobby Gould. And there are many more players like him, who British clubs simply ignore.

Ndlovu, who comes from Zimbabwe, is a rarity in Britain - an African footballer. The only other African to succeed here is Liverpool's Bruce Grobbelaar, who is also from Zimbabwe.

And Gould reckons African stars, like Ndlovu, are every bit as good as the best of British.

"Peter's better than Ryan Giggs," says Gould. "If you watch him day-in and day-out, as I did, it's impossible to argue with that. He's the best player I've ever worked with. The biggest compliment I can give him is that I'd pay to watch him train."

African stars can be difficult to track down. Ndlovu was first spotted by former Coventry player Cyrille Regis, now with Wolves. Regis was on tour with Coventry in Zimbabwe, when he came up against Ndlovu, who scored a hat-trick.

As soon as Coventry got back, big Cyrille told the then manager John Sillett to get Ndlovu over to England. He said he was the best youngster he had seen.

Out of Africa

Ryan Giggs

Eventually Ndlovu arrived in the Midlands and captured a regular spot in the Coventry side in 1992. Despite his success, no British club has followed up Coventry's initiative to bring more talent out of Africa.

In fact, it now seems more likely that British stars will migrate to Africa. Norwich striker Efan Ekoku, born in Manchester but with a Nigerian father, chose to play for World Cup qualifiers Nigeria at international level, rather than England.

When it comes to League football, most African stars seem more at home on the Continent. Abedi Pele, African Footballer of the Year in 1993, has been the most successful. He won the European Cup with Marseille in 1993 and was part of a strikeforce, which included Jean-Pierre Papin, now of Milan, and Chris Waddle, now of Sheffield Wednesday. Pele has since moved on to Lyon.

Anthony Yeboah is the latest African star, he is also from Ghana and plays in Germany for Eintracht Frankfurt, where he is one of the top scorers in the Bundesliga.

When Cameroon almost knocked England out of the World Cup Quarter-Finals in 1990 there was an influx of their stars to Europe and goalkeeper Joseph-Antoine Bell now plays for French side St Etienne while striker Francois Omam Biyick is at Lens.

British clubs show no signs of learning, despite having missed out on world class players in the past.

When Zambia toured Britain back in March this year, no scouts turned-up, which shocked Zambian winger Johnson Bwalya.

"There doesn't seem to be much interest from British clubs," says Bwalya, 26.

But after six years in Europe, playing first in Germany and now with FC Bulle in Switzerland, Bulle is keen for his team-mates to follow his example.

"Back in Zambia some of the players are treated very well by their clubs and they are reluctant to move abroad," he says. "But I've benefitted a great deal from playing in Europe. You get experience of different styles and different tactics. It's made me a better player.

"Eight members of the Zambian team play in Europe and that will help us out qualify for the World Cup.

You really notice the difference when a player has come back from Europe to play for Zambia - they are much more tactically aware."

African players have made their breakthrough into Europe but when will Britain follow their lead.

Nigerian star
Efan Ekoku

John Ebbrell

Everton

NIL SATIS NISI OPTIMUM

Des Walker

Sheffield Wednesday

IT HAS often been said football is a funny old game and when you look at some of the characters the sport has produced you can't really argue.

Goalkeepers have a reputation of being the most barking mad of all.

Veteran 'keeper John Burridge was legendary for doing handstands across the box while Bruce Grobbelaar has never been backwards in coming forwards.

But the guys in green are not the only players who are perhaps a couple of studs short of a boot.

Gazza is the clown prince of all football. His antics at Newcastle, Tottenham and now Lazio are well documented.

The Geordie genius will do anything for laughs. He's dressed up as a clown, tried to run his team-mates over as they left training and when he returned from the World Cup in 1990 he sported a false chest as the team bus paraded back through Luton.

Team-mates, media men and even friends know they are never safe when the man who reached hero status by

crying is on the wind up.

On a TV documentary portraying his recovery from his potentially career-ending knee injury, Gascoigne got up in the middle of the night to creep into a friend's bedroom and chuck a bucket of water all over the sleeping beauty! With friends like that...!

Wimbledon are the prankster kings of football. They make life hell for opponents on the field and for each other off it.

No-one in the dressing room is safe when The Dons are in mischievous mood.

"You never leave anything lying around in the dressing-room because you know it will get nicked," striker Dean Holdsworth admits

"Socks, shoes, shirts, you name it, they go missing if they are left

Football can be a

unny old game!

Just ask the game's top clowns

lying around. It's just about the first thing you learn when you come to the club."

The Crazy Gang image has grown as The Dons have become more of a footballing force and Holdsworth agrees: "When you move to Wimbledon you know what's going to happen, we've got a reputation and we want to keep it up."

And the problems for a new signing start straight away. Holdsworth says: "Our initiation ceremony is a bit different, we take a new boy up to Wimbledon Common and take all his clothes off."

But the Dons hitman claimed no-one ever reacts badly to the ceremony: "They can't really, can they? There's 30 blokes up there and if they didn't like it there would only be more stick in store for them."

Even when players leave the South London club they are still prime targets for the

Bruce Grobbe-laugh

pranksters.

Midfielder Greg Berry left Wimbledon for Millwall in March and was welcomed to the new Den with the theft of his socks and then a fine for stealing a pair of shoes that had been planted in his bag!

Despite Wimbledon's legendary reputation for practical jokes Holdsworth says life in the dressing-room is packed with jokes of the verbal rather than practical type.

"It's almost all banter," he reveals. "We're always giving each other stick and winding each other up but there's actually very little practical joking."

The former Watford and Brentford striker admits there's not one player responsible for the Crazy Gang gimmicks.

"There's 11 jokers in our team and manager Joe Kinnear (left) joins in as well, but obviously there's a line to be drawn with him being the boss. He's one of the lads but also the manager.

"I think that is the secret of our success, we are a team of jokers and we carry that out on to the field. Nobody has got the same team spirit as us," he says.

Former greats Rodney Marsh and George Best are now making a career out of football funnies.

The pair, who once tackled each other when they were playing the same side, toured the country earlier this year with their show: A Sporting Night To Remember. And they had audiences in stitches at every stop in the 18 night run recounting tales from on and off the field.

Best and Marsh are just two of the many comics in football who prove that it can be game for a laugh.

A QUESTION

PICTURE BOARD
Can you identify the mystery men?

1.
2.
3.
4.
5.
6.

Put yourself in Bill Beaumont or Ian Botham's shoes and tackle our quiz based on the popular BBC TV series.

HOME OR AWAY?

HOME:
Which club finished in third place in last season's Premiership?

AWAY:
Which top European award did Roberto Baggio win in 1993?

MYSTERY GUEST

Who is the star having trouble on the ski slopes?

OF SPORT

Compiled by
Steve Pearce

WHAT HAPPENED NEXT?

Study the action picture taken during the 1991 FA Cup Final and tell us what followed.

ONE MINUTE ROUND

You have 60 seconds to answer the following questions

60
45   15
30

1 Who did Mike Walker replace as manager of Everton?

2 For which country does Andrei Kanchelskis play?

3 Middlesbrough play their home games at which ground?

4 From which club did Nottingham Forest sign Stan Collymore?

5 These players could all be found in the park?
a) Michael - (Wrexham) b) Chris - (England)
c) Peter - (Port Vale)

Answers on
page 118

Ray Parlour
product of the Arsenal talent factory!

RAY PARLOUR doesn't exactly look like Bryan Robson, but the flame-haired Arsenal midfielder's style of play has caused many people to mistake him for the genuine article.

That's a difficult comparison for any young player to bear because Robson, the former Manchester United and England captain, can only be described as a winner.

Parlour, 21, is a graduate of one of the most famed academies in England - the Highbury youth programme - which consistently produces players of the highest quality.

As soon as Parlour joined the North London club as a 15-year-old, he knew that his professional ambitions would more than likely be realised.

Arsenal rarely receive youngsters through their famous marble halls who they do not think will make the grade. That's the Highbury way.

Once accepted into the Arsenal fold, youngsters are treated as adults and have very high standards expected of them. They grow up quickly and are expected to succeed.

Parlour is the classic example of this strict regime. As a 20-year-old, he had already won England Under-21 caps, a Coca-Cola Cup winners' medal, and played in an FA Cup Final.

Whereas other big clubs like Blackburn and Manchester United import several million-pound players, Arsenal rarely have to worry themselves about looking outside their own back yard.

That is because they already have home-grown gems of their own. Arsenal are a rich club but they would only spend if they were convinced new players would complement those already at Highbury.

The amount of successful players Arsenal have produced, like Tony Adams, Paul Merson, Paul Davis and David Hillier is far greater than any other club.

Parlour, too, has fulfilled that dream, but is just a proud part of a long tradition. Even if he does not prove to be another Robbo, you can bet that if any club discover one, Arsenal will.

THE BIGGEST decision most top players have to make these days is which club they want to sign for in a multi-million pound deal that will net them a fortune.

But in their teenage years a whole crop of stars gracing the Premiership stage faced a choice that could have cost them the lot.

For they were forced to follow a path in either football or another sport.

Aston Villa star Dwight Yorke would have loved nothing more than to spend last winter in his native Caribbean knocking England's bowlers for six with his best mate, West Indian batsman Brian Lara.

Yorke and Lara were inseparable as kids, playing football and cricket together in Trinidad and could easily be doing each other's jobs now.

Soccer

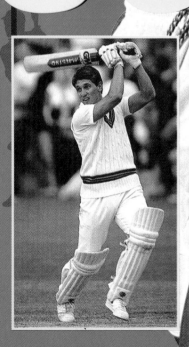

Yorke readily admits that the England bowlers would rather have faced him than the young left-hander who is taking the cricket world by storm.

"I don't think I could have done as well as Brian. He is being talked about as the next Viv Richards and I was never that good.

"Brian was a useful midfielder and I was not too bad as a batsman," Yorke admitted. "We always wanted to be top sportsmen and we struck a bet about who would become more famous.

"I played for Trinidad when I was 17 but I think I made the right choice. I don't think I would ever have made it into the West Indies team and things may not have worked out as well as they have."

"In my schooldays I got a couple of 50s and perhaps one hundred, but I chose football because you are always a lot more involved. In cricket, when you are not batting then you're just sitting around, plus I was better at football!"

Yorke, who signed for Villa in 1989, was a

stars
of other sports

wicketkeeper-batsman in his cricketing days and he admitted: "I guess I'm more in the Jimmy Adams mould than Brian's.

"I used to keep wicket as well as open the batting and I was never a strokemaker like Brian."

But the 22-year-old played down his cricketing credentials, saying: "Most West Indians play both sports. In the rainy season we played football and during the summer we turned to cricket.

"Everyone enjoys both games so it was not unusual. Take Brian, he chose the other option and I'm sure if you asked the current West Indies team there are a few of them who fancy themselves as soccer players."

The summer game almost cost Gary

Lineker (left) a glittering England career. For as a youngster in Leicester it was touch and go whether the golden boy of English football would decide to turn professional in the sport that was his first love.

"When I was a kid I preferred cricket and I was a reasonable player," the former captain of Leicestershire County Cricket Club's boys' team said.

But luckily for English football the man who scored 48 goals for the national side opted for a career with Leicester City rather than donning the whites at Grace Road.

Republic of Ireland Aston Villa star Andy Townsend is another who could easily have slipped through the net as he turned on the style at the snooker tables.

The 31-year-old midfield ace counts his one claim to fame outside of football the day he beat former world snooker champion Joe Johnson.

Townsend's Republic of Ireland colleague Alan Kelly (above) also has a burning ambition away from football.

The Sheffield United keeper said: "My greatest achievement outside of football was when I broke the Lancashire county high jump record and I'd love to win the high jump gold in the Olympics."

And how much sweeter the success enjoyed by Kelly and the others must be for them, knowing they could have opted for a career out of football and made their names in another sport.

Goal Crazy!

ENGLISH soccer has comprised 150,000 fixtures since the Football League came into being in 1888, but two of them remain unique - in differing ways.

One, in December 1892, was and is the only one in which the visiting team scored ten goals - when Sheffield United won 10-0 away to Burslem Port Vale, now Port Vale without the Burslem.

United, then on their way to promotion from the Second Division, included two players who later set individual records: Ernest Needham became the first player to score from a penalty for England, and Rab Howell became the first, and only, gypsy to play for England.

Scoring ten times away is a record that seems likely to stand for another century or so. Even nine by a visiting team is nearly impossible, having been achieved only four times.

The first occasion, in December 1908, was one of the most remarkable matches ever played. Newcastle, having conceded only 13 goals in 15 games, were level 1-1 with Sunderland well into the second half. Sunderland then scored EIGHT times in the last 28 minutes to win 9-1...against the club who went on to win the League championship by a margin of seven points!

The second team to score nine away, Barnsley, did so at Accrington in February 1934. They won the Third Division North title that season, as one of four clubs to score over 100 times, and Accrington, goalless against them, finished 20th as one of four to concede over a century.

There was another unique score on Boxing Day 1938, when Manchester City beat Tranmere 9-3 at Prenton Park in Division Two. City, with the legendary Frank Swift and Peter Doherty in their side, had been champions in 1936-37 but were relegated just twelve months later despite being the First Division's top scorers.

They showed that they had not lost the knack - one more goal against Tranmere would have meant a ton that season, instead of the eventual 99.

The fourth nine-goal feat, equalling Sunderland's First Division best, took place in September 1955, when Cardiff were hammered 9-1 at Ninian Park by a Wolves team with such outstanding players as 1-5-cap Billy Wright (main piicture) and Dennis Wilshaw (above), who earlier that year had become the only Englishman to score four goals in one game against Scotland.

The other divisional away records all involved eight-goal feats - 8-0 by Walsall at Northampton in the old Third South in April 1947, 8-0 by Fulham at Halifax (Third) in September 1969, with Steve Earle (below) scoring five goals, and 8-1 by Rotherham at Crewe (Fourth) in September 1973.

Rotherham then lost nine and drew three of their next 12 away games, and finished 18th.

And, just to prove that these scorelines aren't a freak of the past, Plymouth rattled eight past Hartlepool in the Second Division on the very last day of last season.

Poor old Hartlepool had already been relegated but Peter Shilton's boys had no mercy for them as they ran out 8-1 winners.

So you see it still happens. Beware - it could be your team on the wrong end of a thrashing next term!

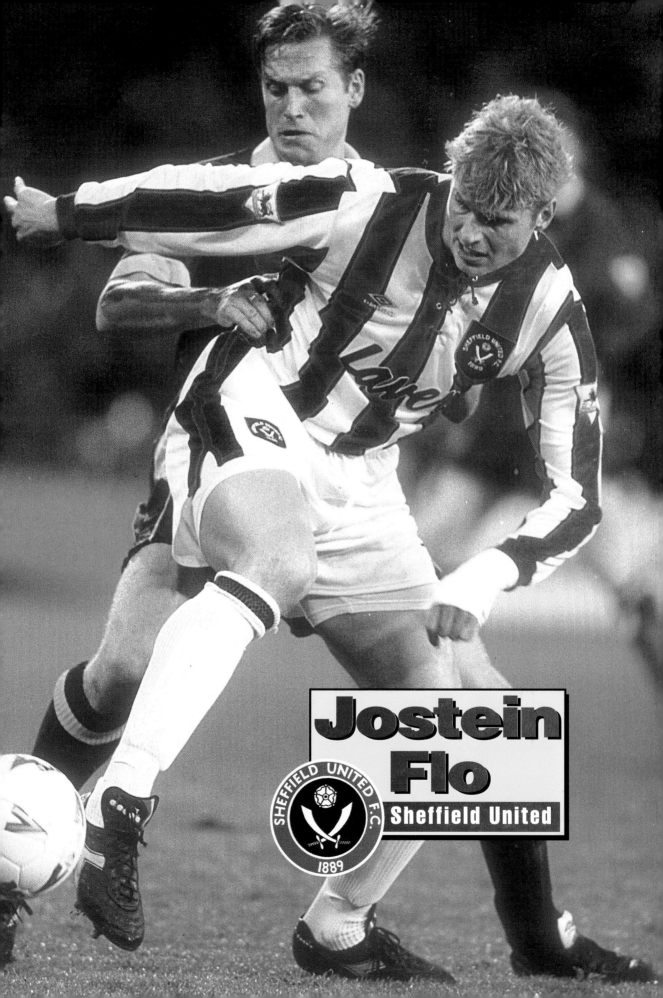

Jostein
Flo
Sheffield United

Many of today's stars are playing for the clubs they once supported

EVERYONE dreams of playing for their favourite team, but few ever manage it. Some even get to play against their heroes and often have their best performances inflicting damage on the team they once supported. These are just some of the great players who have played at the ground where they once stood on the terraces.

Dream

TOTTENHAM striker Terry Sheringham was born and brought up only a little way from White Hart Lane.

As he grew up he used to go with his mates to cheer on the Spurs little knowing that one day they would be there to cheer him on.

"My favourite players included Glenn Hoddle, Ossie Ardiles, Steve Perryman and Steve Archibald. They were in the team that won the FA Cup in 1981 and I believe they were among the best ever.

"When I joined Millwall I kept in touch with my mates and still watched out for Spurs results.

"Then when I joined Forest I played at White Hart Lane and I met up with my mates again. Forest won 2-1 although I didn't score that day.

"When Spurs signed me just after the start of last season it was like coming home."

Many players followed Newcastle as youngsters. Manchester United's Steve Bruce, Blackburn's Alan Shearer, Gazza and many others still look for The Magpies' results.

Only Gascoigne made the grade with the Geordies but there is another of today's stars who was and still is a total Newcastle fanatic and he is one of their star players - Lee Clark.

"I've always been a Magpies' fan and still sometime have to remind myself that I am actually playing and not going to the ground to stand with my mates," he says. "To play for them is fantastic and also to play alongside Peter Beardsley is brilliant. It's a dream come true to be in the same side as him because he's such a special player - one of my idols."

DAVID BATTY used to go along to Elland Road when he was a kid and he always dreamed of being captain of Leeds United one day, his dream came true.

"My dad used to take me to all the matches. He used to take a wooden box for me to stand on s that I could see better," says David.

"When you are a young lad you have all these fancy ideas of being out there with the crowd cheering you on.

"I always wanted to be another Billy Bremner and when I joined Leeds he was there as my boss, giving me lots of tips. Later when we had a few injuries I was

given the captain's armband for a while and that really did fulfil my dream. I'm a Blackburn player now, but I will always be a Leeds fans."

CURRENT Leeds star Gary Speed had a totally different twist to his dream. "My dad was a keen Liverpool fan so to be different I decided I was going to support Everton.

I used to go and see them as often as possible and I thought I would like to play for them.

"Then Leeds offered me a chance so I went to Elland Road. I still kept an eye on the Everton results though. Then came promotion to the First Division and our opening game was away to Everton.

"We won 3-2 and I scored one of our goals. It was a great start to our return to the top division, but why did it have to be Everton!"

COVENTRY international star Peter Ndlovu started his soccer interest back home in Zimbabwe yet the 20-year-old was a keen Liverpool fan and used to watch English football every week on television

"I still think they are a great team and it is a special thrill when I have to play against them. "

ALLY McCOIST never really wanted to play for anyone but Rangers. He was brought up in a houseful of Ibrox fans - the whole family. But it was St Johnstone who gave Ally his big chance in soccer.

"I used to go to Ibrox to cheer the lads on and always wanted to play for them. I never thought I would get the chance. I joined St Johnstone and played for them but in my first couple of seasons I didn't exactly set the world on fire.

"Then I found my goal touch and within a year I was signed by Sunderland - even further from Ibrox. It was party time when Rangers singed me in June 1983. I have been here ever since and I want to stay here for ever.

ASTON VILLA star defender Steve Staunton has had two out of three of his dreams come true.

When he was a lad in Drogheda he dreamed of playing for his two favourite clubs and for his country. He is well on the way to a hat-trick. - IF VILLA would let him!

"I used to follow both Liverpool and Celtic fanatically and I always wanted to play for Ireland.

A Liverpool scout spotted me playing in Ireland and the first part of my dream came true when I made my Liverpool debut in 1987.

"Then in 1988 I won my first full cap for the Republic and that was dream No. 2 come true. I love playing for Villa so I don't suppose I shall ever get dream No 3 but I still watch for the Celtic results."

Teams 6

Spot
the difference

Our computer expert has been messing around with this fab action shot from last season's match between Wimbledon and Southampton. There are five differences in the bottom picture.

The ball has been moved and the sponsorship on Fash's shirt changed, but can you spot the other three changes?

Answers

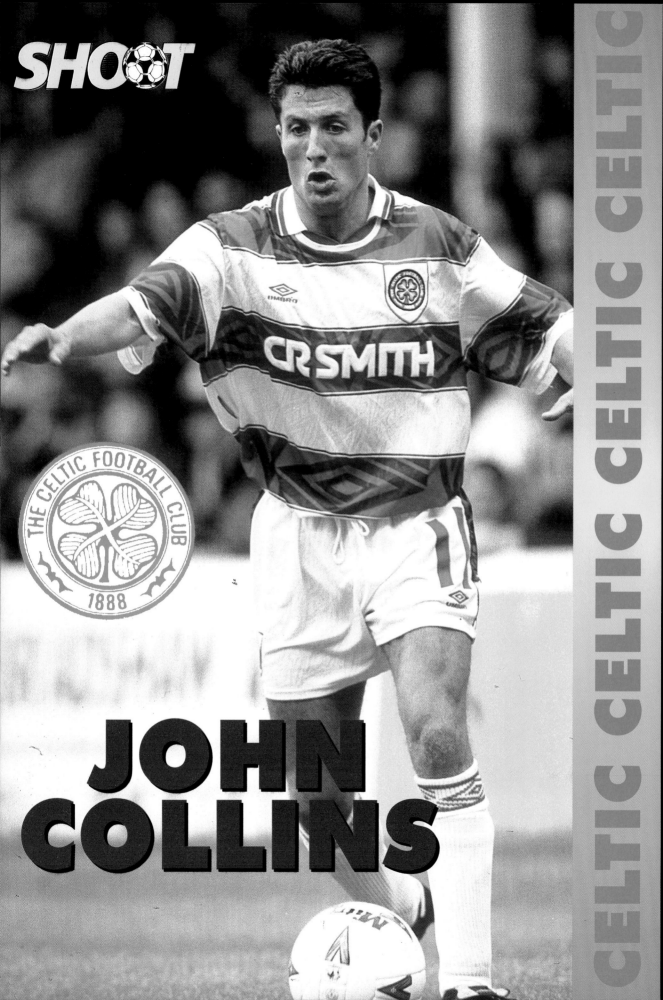

● Script by Stuart Green ● Art by Garry Marshall ● Letters by Steve Pott●

England's Gary Lineker

Gary samples the local dish

A warm welcome from adoring fans

Centre of attention for Grampus Eight

I LOVE ♥ JAPAN

Japan's rising son

The attractive face of Japanese soccer

Gary's appearances were limited due to injury

ONCE upon a time, Gary Lineker was simply a footballer with an eye for goal. Now he is a one-man industry with a lofty reputation in both eastern and western hemispheres.

Since Lineker arrived in Japan in March 1993, the former Leicester, Everton, Barcelona, Spurs and England superstar hasn't played too often because of a broken foot.

But it hasn't stopped him becoming a household name, advertising products on television, becoming a media star and leading Japan's bid to stage the 2002 World Cup.

"I've thoroughly enjoyed my time in Japan, even though it has been frustrating to miss so much football through injury," says Lineker, who will probably retire from football when his contract with Grampus Eight runs out next year.

"The people have been so friendly and football has caught on in an unbelievable way. The marketing of the game has been first-class and I believe Japan would make great World Cup hosts."

Lineker has always enjoyed a challenge. He became one of England's most successful soccer exports during his time with Barcelona.

Unlike some English players, he mastered the language, made new friends and enjoyed the cosmopolitan lifestye.

He returned to England with Spurs an improved player and more confident person. Grampus Eight, based in the city of Nagoya, knew they were getting the perfect ambassador as well as one of the world's top goalscorers when they signed Lineker.

So far they haven't been disappointed. Grampus suffered a poor first season, with Lineker forced by injury to stay on the sidelines. But the public continued to adore him.

"I do get recognised when I go out - so I use it as an excuse not to do any shopping," jokes Lineker.

"Seriously, the interest in me shows how interested people are in the game. Baseball and Sumo used to be the big sports, but now football is rivalling them.

"The reaction from fans has been phenomenal. League games are usually sold out and when Japan went to Spain to train for a World Cup match, 100 journalists and photographers went with them."

Injuries apart - and Lineker was so worried about his foot he flew to Chicago in the United States so he would be fit for his second season which begun in March 1994 - he leads an idyllic life with wife Michelle and sons George and Harry.

"I certainly can't complain," says football's Mr Clean. "I wanted to live somewhere different even though I still see myself returning to England after I retire.

"I see my career in Japan as a challenge, helping the game reach new areas. I was pleased to find out the standard of play isn't bad at all.

"Technically the Japanese players are very good even though they are tactically naive."

The Japanese public are fascinated and impressed by Lineker's manners. He is coming to terms with the notoriously difficult Japanese language and they are impressed with his impeccable dress sense, and courteous behaviour both to his hosts and Michelle.

But they know they won't be able to keep English football's greatest ambassador since Bobby Charlton for ever.

Lineker has plenty of options when considering life after playing football - but all of the likelier ones involve a return home to England.

Paul Gascoigne

Lazio

Trevor Sinclair

Turned down Man. United to join Blackpool

QPR's Trevor Sinclair is a man who knows his own mind.

When he was a schoolboy at the FA School of Excellence, he had the chance to join Manchester United - and instead chose Blackpool.

"United wanted me." he says. "But I knew that every year they released about 15 players. I knew them as good players from my days at the School of Excellence, and they were left struggling to find new clubs. I didn't want to run that risk."

So he joined Blackpool and soon made his mark. Last summer there was a queue of clubs who wanted to sign him, including Manchester City and Blackburn. But Sinclair turned down the big money offers to join QPR - because he wanted to join Gerry Francis.

"I was very impressed with Gerry Francis. I like what he had to say and, having worked with him, I know I made the right decision," says Sinclair. "He is always encouraging you and has the knack of bringing out the best in you."

Sinclair spoke to Kenny Dalglish before he signed for Rangers but he claims: "There was never any question of joining Blackburn. Once I'd met Gerry, I'd made up my mind. He's a top coach who's really brought my game on."

Sinclair, 21, has been a big hit at QPR. He joined at the beginning of last season, when Andy Sinton left for Sheffield Wednesday. That put added pressure on him - Rangers fans were expecting him to live up to Sinton's high standards.

"I never looked on myself as Andy's replacement," he says. "I wanted the fans to accept me as a player in my own right. Andy's a quality player and I'd love to achieve what he has.

"When I arrived at QPR the fans treated me as a young player and they gave me a bit of breathing space."

Sinclair had to learn quickly though. His debut came in Rangers' second game of the season - against Liverpool.

"It was incredible to play in the Premiership, against the top players. Everyday I have to pinch myself to make sure I'm here! "

Training with players like Les Ferdinand and Ray Wilkins is great. You learn so much. Sinclair has now broken into the England Under-21 side, who are coached by Wilkins, and he knows just how good he is.

"His work with the ball is exceptional," says Wilkins. "He will have no problems adapting to the England senior side. I think he'll go to the very top."

IF YOU want to get ahead - get a Scot. That could be the message to clubs who want to follow in the successful footsteps of Manchester United, Blackburn, Arsenal and many others who have found a change of fortune after putting a SuperMac in the hot seat. Just look at some of their achievements.

ALEX FERGUSON

ALEX FERGUSON is almost an opposite to Dalglish. He never won a senior Scottish cap and his playing career, although reaching the top with Rangers, was unspectacular. Yet he has emerged as one of the greatest managers of all time.

Ferguson began his management career very early as he explains:

"I was encouraged by Willie Cunningham who was my boss at both Dunfermline and Falkirk. He pushed me all the time to get into coaching. I had my badge by the time I was 24. When I was 30 he appointed me player-coach at Falkirk. I owe a lot to his encouragement."

Fergie's career took him to Aberdeen and in eight years there he won ten major honours, the highlight being the European Cup-Winners' Cup in 1983. Before taking over the Dons he had been at St Mirren whose fortunes had also been revolutionised under him. But there

was more in store as Rangers, Arsenal and Spurs all tried to tempt him from Pittodrie.

"The Rangers job was very tempting but it was not the job for me. I made my decision on that and have never regretted it," he says.

Fergie became the only manager to win the European Cup-Winners' Cup with two different clubs when United lifted the trophy in 1991. The coveted Championship and the FA Cup have also been attached to his name and the Old Trafford fans see him fast approaching the same legendary status as Sir Matt Busby, who was also a Scot. What is so special about Fergie?

"He has a great will to win," says Denis Law. "He believes in hard work and honest football. He likes players to express themselves and he has that raw Scottish streak of aggression that adds steel to his side and motivates them to get out there and earn their success."

Super Ma

KENNY DALGLISH

KENNY DALGLISH went from being one of the greatest players Scotland has ever produced to being one of the best managers in Britain.

When he pulled on a Scotland shirt for the last time on September 10th, 1986 he won his record 102nd senior cap. Bulgaria were the opponents and the result was 0-0, but the Hampden crowd were saying goodbye to their most-capped player and their joint top-scorer.

Kenny was born in Glasgow on March 4th, 1951. His dad was a keen Rangers fan and took Kenny all over Scotland to see his favourite team. It came as a bit of a shock then when Kenny announced that he was joining Celtic.

It was the start of a fantastic career that saw him play 204 Leagues games and score 112 goals for Celtic before moving to Liverpool in 1978 where he then hit 118 League goals in 355 matches.

During his playing days Dalglish won just about every domestic honour as well as European medals - and before he finished playing he became manager of Liverpool.

As boss of Liverpool, Dalglish did the elusive League and FA Cup double as well as winning various other honours. Then in 1991 he surprisingly left and a little while later he became boss of Blackburn. His success in taking them from the First Division to the pinnacle of the Premier is now in the history books, but what makes him so special? Denis Law gave his opinion:

"Kenny has all the best attributes of a soccer manager - he has been there and done it all. He has a good soccer brain and he knows how to get the best out of his players. I think the fact that he was a player-manager before he hung up his boots worked very well for him.

"It was a gradual transformation. The players were unable to forget what he had already achieved. A successful manager is one who has the greatest respect from his players. "

c Bosses

Super Mac Bosses

GEORGE GRAHAM

GEORGE GRAHAM could be the compromise between swashbuckling Ferguson and dead-pan Dalglish. He is a very thoughtful manager, quite adept at blowing his stack when necessary but also very cool when everyone else is running a high temperature. He was the same as a player.

Although is best remembered for his playing days with Arsenal, he began as an apprentice with Aston Villa, having been tempted from his home near Glasgow to try to carve a career in England. He made his senior debut with Villa in 1963 and later went to Chelsea and had two seasons there before joining Arsenal for a high-profile six years which peaked with the League and Cup double in 1971.

He skippered the side and entered the Highbury Hall of Fame, not knowing then that he would be returning.

From Arsenal, George joined Manchester United then Portsmouth and finally ended his playing days at Crystal Palace where his old pal Terry Venables was manager and soon made George his chief coach.

Graham's career had taken him to many personal honours, including Scottish caps at schools, Under-21 and senior level. His experience was invaluable. In 1982 Graham had the chance to become manager of Millwall and it was the start of a whole new career. He took them from Division Three to the edge of Division One in four years and then came the Arsenal job.

Graham's return to Highbury signalled a revival in The Gunners' fortunes. Two League Championships and cup successes have put them back among the elite of Britain and Europe.

Arsenal have been tagged 'boring', but that is chiefly by the many they have defeated. It is true that Graham is a tactician who expects his players to follow orders but in signing individuals like Ian Wright, George has proved that he does not want a team of robots.

"I expect players to perform to their ability. I believe in tactical plans and we do spend time working on certain situations but that is no different to anyone else. Each game is an individual and plans are made to suit each occasion. We are not just a team of defenders. We have a good defence but we have players with great scoring ability too."

George Graham's golden age of Gunners looks set to roll on for some time, proving him to be another great Scot in the hot seat.

"George is a master tactician and so professional a manager as he was as a player," says Law. "He expects total professionalism from his players but it is unfair to say that he stifles them. He allows them to do what they do best and will organise his team to use their skills. He injects a lot of pride in his players and sets high standards for them."

THREE great Scots with great success records - and there are many others past and present - Bill Shankly, Sir Matt Busby, Bruce Rioch, Tommy Docherty, Lou Macari - to name but a few. Try to think of an English manager who has had the same impact in Scotland. If anyone springs to mind, let us know. So why are the Scots so good? Denis Law explained:

"I think that there is often a greater will to win. There are many great English managers as well but they tend to stay in England. A Scottish manager in this country seems to have that little bit more pride and desire to do well. That's the difference."

1st day

Here is a round-up of some of the unusual things that have happened on day one of various seasons down the years.

1920: Swindon's first-ever League game resulted in a 9-1 win over Luton, still the club's record victory.

1957: Jimmy Greaves made his debut for Chelsea, at 17, scoring in a 1-1 draw at Tottenham - a club he later joined.

1957: Leicester played their first game with England international forward Johnny Morris suspended by the FA after being sent off...in the club's public trial match.

1959: Brian Clough scored three goals in Middlesbrough's 9-0 home win over Brighton. Later in

Tony Cottee strikes

the season he scored another three as Boro won 6-4 in the return match at Brighton.

1962: Alan Ball's debut for Blackpool, who won 2-1 at Liverpool. Over the next 12 seasons, Liverpool won 11 first-day games and drew the other.

1963: Charlton's Keith Peacock became the first substitute used in a League match when he replaced injured keeper Paul Rose at Bolton, who won 4-2.

1969: Charlie George made his debut for Arsenal, against Everton.

1970: George broke an ankle, also against Everton.

1971: Kevin Keegan, a £35,000 buy from Scunthorpe, made his debut for Liverpool and scored the first of exactly 100 goals he netted for the club before moving to Hamburg.

1972: Leeds lost 4-0 at Chelsea after goalkeeper David Harvey and striker Mick Jones had been carried off in the first 26 minutes.

1974: Chelsea unveiled their new £2 million stand, and lost 2-0 at home to Carlisle, who were playing their first game as a First Division club.

1976: Charlie George, now playing for Derby, was sent off against Newcastle.

1977: Wimbledon played their first match as a League club. Their team included one of the oldest debutants ever - 35-year-old David Donaldson.

1977: Tranmere Rovers began the season by using the same 11 players they called on for the next 27 League games as well. Only the substitutes were changed.

1977: Paul Hooks went on as Notts County substitute at Blackburn...and was sent off three minutes later.

1980: England defender Dave Watson, transferred from Manchester City to Werder Bremen, played his first game in Germany...and was sent off.

1983: Geoff Palmer of Wolves scored from a penalty in the first minute of a 1-1 draw against Liverpool - the only goal he claimed all season.

1986: Middlesbrough had to start their season at Hartlepool, and drew 2-2 with Port Vale. Boro's own ground had been barred to them by the Official Receiver - but they survived and are still in the League.

1986: Graeme Souness, making his debut as player-manager of Rangers, against Hibs, was sent off and eight others were booked.

1987: Scarborough's first League match finished 15 minutes later than the rest because of a pitch invasion by visiting Wolves fans.

1988: Tony Cottee, bought from West Ham for a record £2.2 million, scored a hat-trick for Everton against Newcastle. John Aldridge also scored three, for Liverpool at Charlton.

1991: Barnet played their first ever match in the Fourth Division and lost 7-4 at home to Crewe. "I thought they were going to get 20," said Barnet manager Barry Fry.

1993: Mick Quinn of Coventry scored an opening-day hat-trick against Arsenal...five years after scoring one for Newcastle against Leeds.

The young Jimmy Greaves

Mick Quinn

Star soccer wives

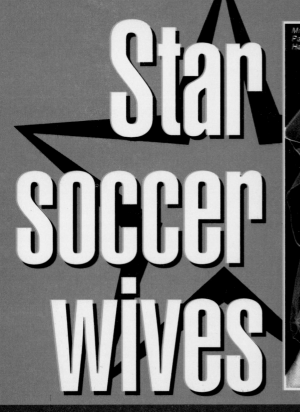

Mr and Mrs Pat Van den Hauwe.

FOOTBALLERS are used to having their names chanted on the terraces - but their wives? Now that is a novelty.

The fame of Mrs Pat Van den Hauwe, alias model Mandy Smith, is such that fans know as much about her as they do about her footballing husband.

Mick McCarthy, Van den Hauwe's manager at Millwall, cannot understand why the wife of one of his players attracts so much attention.

"What has Pat's wife got to do with football? My wife doesn't get a mention," says McCarthy.

But McCarthy does not realise that one of his star players is part of one of football's select band of celebrity couples.

Lee Chapman and the lovely Leslie Ash.

West Ham striker Lee Chapman and his wife, actress Leslie Ash are another star couple but they prefer to stay out of the headlines.

Former England midfielder Neil Webb has witnessed the emergence of his wife Shelley into a celebrity in her own right.

She has appeared often on BBC TV's 'Standing Room Only' and also writes for newspapers such as 'The Daily Telegraph'.

Mandy Smith is used to fame having been married to former Rolling Stone Bill Wyman.

Even her divorce from the rock star did not stop her desire to be in the public eye.

Pat may not have the world-wide fame of Bill Wyman, but in English football he is legendary for his crunching tackles.

The couple showed no signs of wanting to keep out of the limelight when they got married in the most glitzy of showbiz weddings.

In June 1993 the world's photographers turned up to catch a few shots of Pat and Mandy's fairytale wedding.

By October, Mandy had brought out her autobiography, 'It's All Over Now'.

The glare of publicity has its draw backs. Van den Hauwe was forced to miss two games for Millwall with a back injury after he battled against an intruder.

The thief made away with thousands of pounds worth of jewellery.

To avoid putting herself under unnecessary spotlight, Mandy is not a regular visitor to The New Den to watch her husband play for Millwall.

She enjoys the fact that Pat is often away travelling with the team. "We do like our own space," says Mandy. "When Pat goes to work I have time to myself - but I'm always glad to see him when he comes home. We always look forward to being in each other's company."

Pat has had a 'wildman' image ever since his days with Everton where he won medals galore under Howard Kendall.

But he believes he has calmed down since he got married to Mandy. "Mandy came into my life at just the right time and Millwall fans can expect to see me around at the Den for a long time to come," says Pat.

When Neil Webb moved from Nottingham Forest to Old Trafford, his wife Shelley had to make a big decision about her own career as a journalist.

She says; "I didn't want to leave Nottingham for Manchester, but I knew that the move was so important to Neil so I'm not complaining. It's a short career and he has to do what is right for him."

Although Shelley is now a TV personality in her own right she has not always enjoyed such independence.

"My father once introduced me as Neil Webb's wife and I kicked him in the shin," she says.

Mandy Smith rarely watches her husband playing for Millwall.

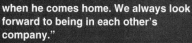
Shelley Webb ... TV journalist.

Husband Neil ... soccer star.

Viking Invasion

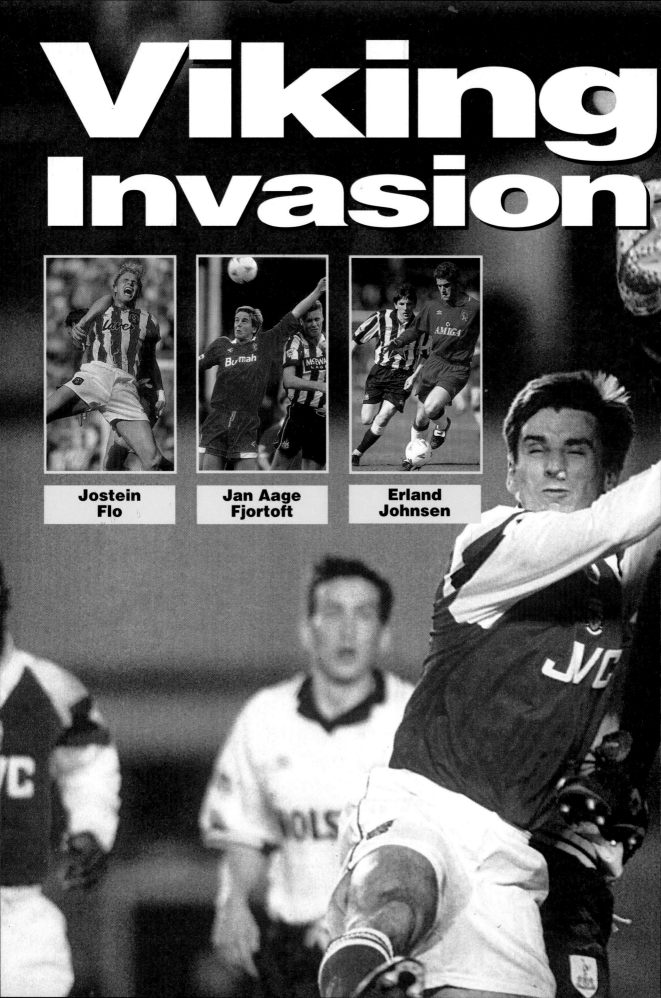

Jostein Flo

Jan Aage Fjortoft

Erland Johnsen

The Vikings are back

But this time there are no long boats or horned helmets, it's all football boots and goalkeeping gloves.

Gone are the days when Premiership managers looked to South America to bring in their foreign stars. Now the top bosses set their sights on the untapped lands of Norway, Iceland and Denmark.

Of all the countries from soccer's Scandinavian outposts, it is the Norwegians who have found the flight path to Britain with the greatest ease.

Erik Thorstvedt, Erland Johnsen, Gunnar Halle, Jostein Flo and Jan Aage Fjortoft are just a few of the players who have made their mark in the Premiership.

The Norsemen love it over here and, despite a few teething problems, they are proving to be some of England's top imports.

Thorstvedt is the most established name from the other side of the North Sea and when he joined Spurs in 1989 he fulfilled a dream.

"I had always wanted to play in England and I knew Spurs were one of the top clubs," he says.

And he has nothing but admiration for football away from the fjords. "There have always been close links between Norway and England, and quite a few people come over to watch the games here," he admits.

"We used to have English matches televised live on Saturday afternoons until they experimented by showing games from the Bundesliga on alternate weeks. But people were unhappy with the standard of German football and it was soon dropped."

Thorstvedt's dream almost ended before it began. When he made his debut he dropped a massive clanger by letting a soft 25-yarder from Nigel Clough through his hands in a live game at Nottingham Forest.

"I wanted to dig a huge hole and jump into it," he admits. "That goal was treated as a minor disaster in my home town."

Since then, however, the only way has been up for Thorsvedt. He collected an FA Cup medal in 1991 and is now a firm favourite with the fans.

The 6ft 4inch giant wants to see his career out with Tottenham and puts the transformation from 'Erik the 'Orrible' to 'Viking Great' down to his coming to terms with the physical side of the game and the added intensity.

"The physical side of the English game takes some getting used to," admits the 31-year-old keeper.

"In the Spurs dressing room, the lads are mickey-taking 45 minutes before kick-off. But just before we go out, their eyes are popping out of their heads. They're so psyched up and everyone pulls together. I think it's unique to England."

The adjustments to the English game mean that very rarely do the Norwegian imports grab the headlines from day one, a fact which makes it very difficult for them to settle in immediately.

No-one typifies that more than Swindon's Jan Aage Fjortoft, who joined the West Country side from Rapid Vienna last year.

In the early months, life in England was one long nightmare for the striker as he looked like a fish out for water. He came within an ace of taking the trip back across the North Sea, but then he finally found the back of the net and hasn't looked back.

"I had almost booked my ticket back to Lillestrom...then I got a goal," Fjortoft says. "It just wasn't going for me.

"I wondered whether I should change my game and I was looking at other strikers but I decided to play my way."

And how that decision has paid off. Fjortoft is firing on all cylinders and life in Wiltshire is a happy one for the 27-year-old.

Chelsea centre-half Erland Johnsen sums up the feelings of the Premiership's Norwegian contingent when he says: "We all grew up watching English football and that's the way we love to play. It's the league everyone wants to play in."

The 27-year-old tough-tackling defender spent 18 months at Bayern Munich but admits: "We played a man to man system there and it didn't suit me. The English game is my kind of game and that's why I'm sure that the Norwegian players have done so well over here.

"Added to that is the fact that English is our second language so it is easier for us as opposed to players from other countries - that helps you settle in quicker."

Johnsen admits his decision to turn his back on Norway's domestic programme has almost certainly hindered his international chances, but he adds: "It was my decision to go to Germany and then to England and I haven't regretted it. I would probably have played more times for Norway if I had been playing for one of their premier teams - but I couldn't miss the opportunity of playing in England. It's the only place to play."

> The Norsemen making their mark in Britain

Tottenham's Norwegian giant Erik Thorstvedt

Honest Andy

Hot-shot

PFA Young Player of the Year and SHOOT/adidas Golden Shoe winner Andy Cole was the toast of Newcastle last season when he broke a goalscoring record created nearly 70 years ago. Hot-shot Cole hit 41 goals which is more in one season than any other Newcastle player.

"I was not surprised at scoring so many goals last season. I've always had confidence in my own ability and being part of a team that creates so many chances, it is not difficult to score.

"I practise shooting, heading, positioning and all the other things you need to score goals, but a lot of it comes is confidence and if you have faith in yourself and your team-mates you won't go far wrong. I can't deny that you need a share of luck as well.

"Having a manager like Kevin Keegan to work with has helped to improve my play. He has worked on all aspects of my game. He was a striker so he understands what makes a player in my position tick. He also ensures I keep my feet on the ground and don't get too carried away by all the media hype.

"My ambitions know no boundaries. I believe Newcastle can make a very serious challenge for the Championship this season and open the door to the European Cup. I want to win every honour possible with The Magpies.

"If I continue to score goals I hope my chance of a regular England place will follow."

DID YOU KNOW THAT?

Andy was born in Nottingham on October 15th, 1971.
❚His first club was Arsenal - he joined them as a schoolboy. He played just one senior game for them.
❚His nickname is "Andy Goal"
He is a music nut and has a great collection of CDs. He also likes to dance and to go to concerts.
He wants to play in Italy one day -when he has achieved all he wants with Newcastle.

Cole

Hughie Gallagher the Great

IT was Hughie Gallagher who established the Newcastle scoring record in 1926-27. He hit 36 in the League and three in the FA Cup. Gallagher was only 5ft 5in, but played 19 times for Scotland and joined Newcastle from Airdrie in 1926 for £6,500. One season he turned down a Scottish cap so that he could play for Newcastle in a vital League match.

George Robledo made history

GEORGE ROBLEDO matched Gallagher's record in the 1951-52 season. He was a Chilean international who came to this country in 1946 and scored a hat-trick on his debut for Barnsley against Nottingham Forest. He joined Newcastle in 1948, followed a year later by his brother Edward. They made history in the 1952 FA Cup Final when they both played against Arsenal. George hit the winner. He hit 39 goals that season, including one four-goal haul and three hat-tricks.

Wor Andy?

CAN Andy Cole become Newcastle's greatest ever scorer? To do that he must beat the feat of Jackie Milburn. In his ten seasons at St James's from 1946 to 1957, "Wor Jackie" hit 200 senior goals. Cole is well on his way to becoming a new legend - "Wor Andy".

ASTON VILLA fans were ecstatic after their heroes defeated red-hot favourites Manchester United 3-1 to lift the Coca-Cola Cup at Wembley last season. Is that victory the start of something big for The Villains? Has Ron Atkinson marshalled his troops for an era of triumph, or is there still a lot of work to be done at Villa Park? What IS the future for Aston Villa?

Villa thriller
Dean Saunders

BIG RON'S MASTER PLAN FOR VILLA!

BEFORE Big Ron Atkinson took charge at Villa Park, there was an air of depression around the club. Graham Taylor had been the boss from 1987 to 1990 and he had restored their prestige as a top division side and even steered them to runners-up place in the old First Division before he left to take over as England supremo.

Dr Josef Venglos was his replacement and the Villa fans suffered a disappointing season. The team narrowly avoided relegation and were bombed out of the UEFA Cup. Just as a period of glory seemed within grasp, it escaped. Then came Ron Atkinson.

He took over in June 1991, having just steered Sheffield Wednesday back to the First Division and won the League Cup - ironically at the expense of his old club Manchester United. The Wednesday fans were angry at his departure - the Villa fans were delighted at his arrival.

There was work to be done and a challenge that Ron - himself once a Villa player - relished. Money was available, but it had to be spent wisely. The essence of that wisdom was seen in signing Cyrille Regis on a free transfer. That meant money saved to be spent on stars like Dalian Atkinson, Dean Saunders,

Steve Staunton, Ray Houghton, Earl Barrett, Kevin Richardson, Shaun Teale, Garry Parker and Mark Bosnich. Truly, today's Aston Villa is the team that Ron built.

When Manchester United won the first Premiership title in 1993, Villa finished second. Ron was disappointed. His masterly tactics paid off in the 1994 Coca-Cola Cup Final, but he was again disappointed at his side's Premier placing. A European challenge is fine, but Ron wants something he has never won - the Premier Championship; and the key to the European Cup.

"I think I have won all the other domestic honours and I know what it is like to compete in Europe," says Big Ron. "Winning the FA Cup and the League Cup gives you a great sense of satisfaction, but winning the Championship and knowing that it is the

Andy Townsend and Tony Daley enjoy that winning feeling

result of a nine-month campaign in which you have emerged as the best team in the land must be every manager's dream.

"That cake is great enough, but the icing comes when you compete in the European Cup as Champions. That's something I would like."

Ron often has the image of being a big-spender and it is true that he is not afraid to splash out, but it is often forgotten that he is also prepared to sell. During his first two years at

Villa, he spent £9.9 million but he also gained £10.1 million in sales. He threatened that if his side did not improve during the latter part of last season he would be doing a lot more selling.

"I have to do what I think is right for Aston Villa. This club has been going for about 120 years and a lot of players - and managers - have been and gone in that time.

"The club is still there. I will do whatever I think is necessary to benefit Aston Villa and if it means selling big names, I will do it.

"I never sell for the sake of it or buy for the sake of it. I have never been a panic merchant. I always seek to buy or

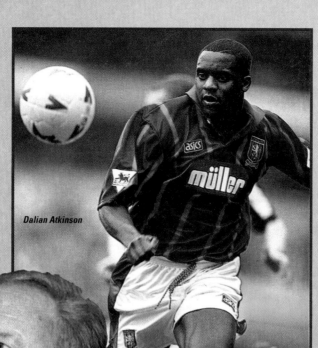

Dalian Atkinson

sell at a fair price."

But where do Villa go from here? Is the present squad good enough to make Ron's Premiership title dream come true?

"We have a squad of class players. We also have a very strong nucleus of young players coming through and the combination of the two means that we have a good present and a good future. That does not mean to say that this is it, that we have the squad

that we need and that I am happy with that. Not at all.

"You can have the best players in the country, but that does not mean that they are going to be compatible. Sometimes you have to make changes that on paper seem a little strange. But the people who look at the paper are not there at the training ground or know whether the performance in the match is anything like the performance that has been talked about beforehand.

"I shall never be totally satisfied with what I have. That would be dangerous. It would stop me seeking new ideas, new options. As I see it, Aston Villa has a very good squad of players and I think we are capable of winning anything that is in front of us.

"I don't like to make predictions, they have a bad habit of being taken out of context and then blowing up in your face.

"The plan is to keep the squad we have, more or less, add or subtract as the strengths or weaknesses show themselves and keep pressing towards the Championship. If we pick up any other silverware along the way that will be a bonus, but we are really seeking the title.

"The UEFA Cup can do us a big favour because it can give us something to keep us fresh. It provides a different sort of challenge and means that we get a break from the domestic scene.

"In short, the future for Aston Villa is to be Premier League Champions of England!"

Shaun Teale

Brains in Boots

Kasey Keller - No.1 in our Brain Box X1

Today's footballers are concerned about the length of time they spend at the top and although some earn as much as £10,000 a week the cash can run out well before their 40th birthday.

In the 1970's Steve Heighway and Steve Coppell were famous as two of the only footballers with degrees but now the English Leagues are graced with philosophy, chemistry and mathematics graduates.

SHOOT has taken a look at the brainpower of today's players and picked a Brainy XI that would grace any ground or University Challenge.

Goalkeepers are supposed to be half-mad, but the choice of the No.1 in the Brainy XI came down to two American imports - Jurgen Sommer of Luton and Millwall's Kasey Keller, who both took the traditional US route into sport via a University.

Kasey, who is studying racism in sport as part of a sociology degree, talks about the game in lofty terms and his keen brain means he is actually thinking long and hard about the chants coming from the terraces.

"I just can't understand the racist chanting," he says. "When an opposing black player fouls one of our players you hear cries such as black this and that. But when Millwall's Etienne Verveer (who is black) is in possession he is held as a hero."

Kasey says such things would never

The Brain-Box Team

1. Kasey Keller
2. Barry Horne
3. Jakob Kjeldbjerg
4. Mark Shail
5. David Wetherall
6. Pat Nevin
7. Brian McClair
8. Rick Holden
9. Eric Cantona
10. John Fashanu
11. Iain Dowie

FOOTBALLERS are rarely known for their academic qualities. But the 1990's is breeding a different kind of player, some who are more at home with a copy of War and Peace than The Beano.

be tolerated in his native America, he adds: "I couldn't imagine Michael Jordan going up to slam dunk the ball in the basketball net and the crowd racially abusing him."

Brainpower in the Brainy XI is not in short supply at the back where graduates are thick on the ground.

Mark Shail recently graduated from Surrey University before getting the captaincy at Bristol City while Dane Jakob Kjeldbjerg interrupted a law degree to take his place in the centre of Chelsea's defence.

Swedish born Shail was a part-time sales representative and played for Yeovil before being snapped up by Bristol.

His ability with the pen doesn't however stop him receiving his fair share of trouble on the pitch - "I had my nose broken five times in non-League football," says Shail, who attended Southlands College.

As a part-time player in the Danish First Division (The Super League) last season, Jakob Kjeldbjerg was also studying for a law degree at the nearby Aarhus University.

"I chose to go to University because you can't be a footballer for ever ," said Jakob, who claims that he never gets any stick from the other Chelsea players.

In Denmark he easily balanced both lifestyles as it was the norm in the First Division.

"It wasn't a problem doing both - I used to go to the university in the morning and train in the afternoon," Jakob says "but when I got the chance to come to Chelsea I had only completed nine months of my course, after doing a General Studies degree the year before."

And he hasn't given up on returning to

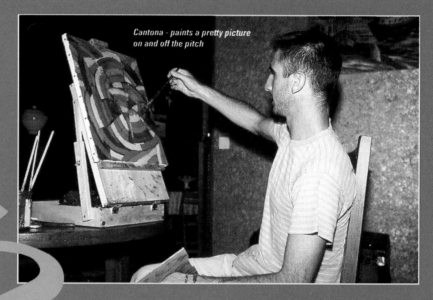
Cantona - paints a pretty picture on and off the pitch

his degree when his playing days are over.

"I still have the books," Jakob says "and I may return to it when my football days are over."

The full-backs in the brain box bunch will have plenty to talk about at half time as both are chemistry students.

David Weatherall played four games for Leeds last season while completing his degree at the university and Welsh international Barry Horne started his career at Rhyl, combining tough-tackling with a chemistry degree at Liverpool University.

Tactical systems would naturally be complicated in the Brain XI but we have gone for a simple three in midfield.

Who better to fly down the right wing than socialist Pat Nevin who is just at home at the Royal Shakespeare Company as on the wing for Tranmere Rovers.

Pat (left), who has a love of music and the arts says, "there's no reason why, just because you play football you shouldn't have normal interests."

And in Pat's case these normal interests involved reading all the classics in his five-year spell at Chelsea and spending nearly all his spare money on theatre tickets and books.

"Some people say that I look down on other players," Pat adds "but I feel they

are misjudged - footballers are some of the most intelligent people I've ever met." Pat, like Jakob Kjeldbjerg, interrupted a degree course to sign for Chelsea, the Scot was studying Business Studies.

Manchester United's Brian McClair, the holder of a degree in Movement Studies, fills the centre of midfield while one of the best crosses in the game, Rick Holden is on the other wing.

Rick joined Halifax in 1986 while still taking a degree course at Carnegie College in Leeds and often took other players, including skipper Phil Brown, to student parties and events.

Rick, now playing for Oldham, used his signing-on fee for Halifax to pay off his student debts and is said to have led Halifax's karaoke nights, on the guitar.

The mercurial Eric Cantona enjoys the works of the poet Rimbaud as much as the team talks of Manchester United manager Alex Ferguson and has shown many in English football that the game can go hand in hand with culture and the arts.

In his recent autobiography Eric said: "An artist, in my eyes, is someone who can lighten up a dark room.

"I never have and will never find any difference between the pass from Pele to Carlos Alberto in the Final of the World Cup in 1970 and the poetry of the young Rimbaud."

Southampton forward Iain Dowie, who has a degree in mechanical engineering and worked as a missile engineer at British Aerospace before starting his career at 23, would fit nicely alongside Cantona in the scholars selection with the team being completed by one of the United Nations' newest ambassadors John Fashanu.

Fashanu spent much of his spare time in Africa on behalf of the United Nations's children's fund UNICEF. Fashanu, who has hosted a television show and runs four companies, worth millions says: "When I first saw poverty in Africa it was heartbreaking...I had to try to do something about it."

Soccer Master

SO you think you know a fair bit about football - well, see how you get on with our Mastermind Test of Soccer Knowledge.

Answers on page 118

COUNTRIES

1. Which country did Argentina beat in a play-off to reach the World Cup Finals?
2. Faustino Asprilla plays for which country?
3. Which country will host the 1998 World Cup Finals?
4. Who won the very first World Cup in 1930?
5. Three countries qualified for the World Cup Finals for the first time in 1994. How many can you name?

PLAYERS

1. Name the player who has had two spells with Millwall, two spells with Tottenham and one spell each with Southampton and Liverpool. You'll have to be sharp to get this one.
2. Which famous goalkeeper began his career with Wolverhampton, but is not related to a great former player of the same name? England could do with a whole bunch of players like this one.
3. This player began his career with his brother at Norwich, but is best known for his eight seasons with a London club. He has played for England twice and he is often on TV not playing football. Who is he?
4. A famous son of a famous dad, he was the first Englishman to win a special award last season. Full marks if you can name him.
5. He played for Manchester United, but not in the League and had two spells in Canada. Now he is with his current Premier League club for the second time. Who is he?

MANAGERS

1. Which manager nicknamed Mark Hughes "Sparky".
2. Who was manager of Rangers before Walter Smith?
3. Who was Chelsea manager before Glenn Hoddle (left)?
4. Ossie Ardiles has been manager of four clubs. How many can you name?
5. Where was Lou Macari manager before he joined Celtic?

CLUBS

1. For which two foreign clubs did Mark Hughes (right) play?
2. Which Scottish club plays at Tynecastle?
3. From whom did Newcastle buy Andy Cole ?
4. Which Northern club are nicknamed The Shakers?
5. Which four clubs reached the FA Cup Semi-Finals last season?

INTERNATIONAL STARS

1. Which Parma player (left) is a Swedish international?
2. Which Norwegian star joined Sheffield United last season?
3. Coventry have a Zimbabwe international in their side - who is he?
4. A well-known German star enjoyed a good season with Monaco. Can you name him?
5. Who was European Footballer of the Year last season?

Le Saux's Wembley Dream

The first Channel Islander to play for England talks about his part in Blackburn's success story and his rise from Chelsea cast-off

Graeme Le Saux is the most promising left-back in England.

The Jersey-born blonde is strong in the tackle, lightning in attack and the ideal role model for the modern defender.

But it has not been a straightforward progression from playing for representative Jersey sides, to Chelsea at 19, then Blackburn and now England.

Le Saux says: "My father, Pierre, is mad on football and I started playing as soon as I could walk. According to him, I watched a Cup Final on television when I was seven and said: 'I'm going to play at Wembley one day.'"

Le Saux attracted interest from French side Caen at 13 and was lined up for a soccer scholarship to an American University at 17, but neither plan came off.

When he was 19, he was spotted by the then Chelsea manager John Hollins, on a business trip to Jersey, and invited for a trial at Stamford Bridge. "Hollins was sacked within months of my arrival and replaced by Bobby Campbell. I was shocked, but it was an early lesson in the workings of pro football," he says.

"I sometimes wonder when I look back at the roads I could have taken in my life. I was very upset when the Caen and American deals didn't come off, but I wouldn't change a thing. I'm having the time of my life at Blackburn."

Campbell was replaced by Ian Porterfield, then came David Webb. All recognised Le Saux's promise, by then an Under-21 and twice capped 'B' international, but failed to get the best out of him.

"I love the football and social life in Blackburn. Moving from Jersey to London was a harder step to take and now that I've got a steady girlfriend, life seems even better."

Under threat

LE SAUX swapped the bright lights of London for life up North when he left Chelsea at the beginning of 1993 to play under Kenny Dalglish at Blackburn Rovers.

With the mega-bucks backing of chairman Jack Walker, money is not object to their quest for success.

But Le Saux reveals that there is no room for complacency at Ewood Park:

"The standards set at this club are so high. We're lucky to have the money when we need it, but it means every player's position is constantly under threat."

The message is simple - one bad game and you're out.

"It's gone too far and reached a point at Blackburn where we have to try and win something every season.

"The amount of money and effort that has gone into building the club means that we have reached the point of no return.

"All the players know that if we don't bring the club success or play well we could be shown the door.

"But I'd never knock it because it is making better players of us I'm certainly playing the best football of my career and am trying harder than ever.

"I've realised that I've been giving more than ever on a football pitch. Because everyone around you has such high standards, you subconsciously make that extra effort to win every ball.

England Shock

LE SAUX discovered he had been selected for his first ever England squad when he is driving around London on a day-off.

He was on his way to visit an old friend when he had to pull over and take a call on his mobile phone and was given the good news by manager Kenny Dalglish.

"I was aware of the speculation about a possible call-up, but it was different to hear it officially," he says.

And Le Saux became the first Channel Islander to win full England honours when he took the field for the 1-0 win over Denmark.

"It was a great feeling and a compliment to both myself and the rest of the Blackburn team because I would be no-one without the other lads, Le Saux adds.

"I'm glad Matt Le Tissier came on too because we have been old rivals since school days. The inter-island matches were special games and Matt was always their main player to watch out for."

Le Saux was signed for Rovers by Dalglish in a £500,000 move from Chelsea - a deal which brought an end to an unhappy spell in his career.

"I was constantly played in different positions at Chelsea and consistency at Blackburn has been the biggest single factor in my improvement and progression to the international scene."

How they began

ARSENAL began life as a result of factory workers at Woolwich Arsenal - makers of ammunition - deciding to start their own football team. That was back in 1886 and they were first called Dial Square because that is the exact spot where they worked. What is really interesting is that two of their players were former Nottingham Forest men and they wrote to their old club asking for some kit. Forest obliged and that is why Arsenal wear red as their main colour.

BLACKBURN ROVERS began life among the upper crust. The club was formed in 1875 as a result of a meeting of Public schoolboys. Cricket and rugby were already on the boys' schedule but they wanted to rough it a little with a game of soccer. Their first Football League game came 13 years later when they gained a home draw on their debut against Accrington Stanley. The result was 5-5.

ASTON VILLA began as a result of a team of cricket enthusiasts of Villa Cross

HAVE you ever wondered how your favourite team was started? Perhaps they were a rowing club or played hockey, were a team of schoolteachers or factory workers. Some clubs began life as a result of an argument. Whatever the reason, every club has a tale to tell - here are some of them.

Wesleyan Chapel wanting to play something in the winter. When the club was formed in 1873 there was a shortage of opposition so for their very first game they played against Aston Brook St. Mary's Rugby Club. They played one half soccer and the other half rugby (below)!

CHELSEA was formed to stop Stamford Bridge from being sold to the railway. In 1904, Mr. Harold Mears wanted to develop his site as a football ground. He offered Fulham the chance to play at

Stamford Bridge but they turned him down. The Great Western Railway wanted to buy the ground as a coal-yard but sports-loving Mr Mears was determined to keep the site for soccer and decided to start his own club. Chelsea were born.

RANGERS began life as a rowing club. The Glasgow club wanted to keep fit and have a bit of fun on dry land as well as continuing their successes on the water. They chose soccer and, in 1873, Rangers began a life that has made them probably the most successful club in the world, having won more domestic honours than anyone else.

MANY clubs have been started as a result of church organisations wanting to play soccer but **LIVERPOOL** were formed out of a disagreement rather than wanting to be together. When Everton left Anfield after a dispute with their landlord in 1892, Mr John Houlding was so annoyed that he decided to form his own club. The rivalry between the two major Mersey sides has been intense ever since.

RAILWAY workers formed **MANCHESTER UNITED** back in 1878. They were known as Newton Heath L and YR Cricket and Football Club. There were turbulent times ahead including bankruptcy before the name

The birth of a club can sometimes be stranger than fiction

Manchester United was adopted in 1902. Their first Football League match took place in 1892 when they travelled to Blackburn for a First Division game and were beaten 4-3.

CELTIC were started to raise some cash for needy families. Unlike their rich neighbours Rangers, Celtic were born out of necessity. The plight of many poor Irish Catholic families who had moved to Glasgow led to some church leaders organising a football team to raise money for them (below right). It worked and Celtic are still going strong 116 years later.

MILLWALL started life in 1885 as Millwall Rovers. They are another club which was formed by factory workers. These were a little different though because they made jam and marmalade. Fortunately they didn't come to a sticky end!

COVENTRY CITY started out in 1883. The club was formed by workers at the Singer cycle factory. When they wanted something to do socially, they decided to get off their bikes and play soccer (above). It was in 1919 that they played their very first League game, a Second Division match against Tottenham. Coventry lost 5-0.

NOTTINGHAM FOREST are one of the oldest clubs in the game. They began life in 1865 but didn't actually play soccer at first. They played a game called shinty, a kind of hockey still enjoyed in parts of Scotland. Determined to play soccer though, the Forest players were given their first kit which turned out to be a set of red caps. Hopefully that is not all they wore or else they would have all needed long beards!

NOTTS COUNTY are generally accepted as being the oldest professional football club in the world, having been started in 1862. The club had played most sports before giving soccer a go. If their start was unspectacular, their first real game was one for the history books as they played against Everton and lost 2-1.

PRESTON can also claim to be one of the oldest clubs in the world. They began life in 1863 but got really serious about football in 1881. In one of their first matches of that year they played against Blackburn Rovers and lost 16-0!

BOTH **SHEFFIELD UNITED** and **WEDNESDAY** were formed from cricket clubs. There was county cricket at Bramall Lane long before The Blades were formed in 1889, while Wednesday got their name for the obvious reason. They were formed in 1867 by the Sheffield Wednesday cricket club, so called because they played their matches on Wednesdays.

SOUTHAMPTON were born out of Deanery FC, a club which was started by schoolteachers who were members of a young mens' association connected to the local St Mary's Church. Southampton was officially founded in 1885. They twice reached the FA Cup Final before even joining the League in 1920.

MANY stories and many beginnings but one of the strangest must be **WREXHAM,** the oldest club in Wales. Wrexham began in 1873 when a group of businessmen formed a team just for one match against the Provincial Insurance, a 17-a-side affair. The team stayed together and Wrexham was born. But it took 12 months before they reduced to 11-a-side!

David

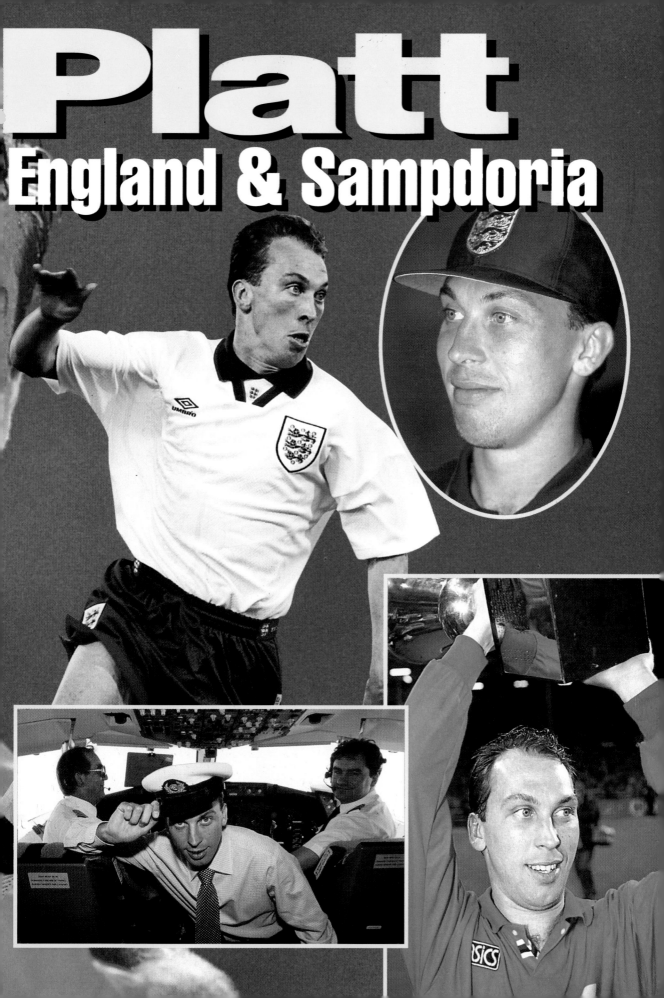

Platt
England & Sampdoria

YOU are a goal down in injury time and you get a penalty. But who is calm enough to take the spot-kick? It takes a pretty cool customer at the best of times, but when the heat is really on, it takes a penalty-king to whack the ball into the net. Here are some of the best in the business.

PETER BEARDSLEY -
The Newcastle hero has taken dozens of penalties in his great career and rarely misses. When team-mate Andy Cole was chasing his record-breaking 40th goal, the Magpies were awarded a penalty against Aston Villa. But it was Beardsley who had the job of taking the kick because a cool head was needed. Needless to say, the England star scored.

GORDON STRACHAN -
When Leeds are awarded a penalty, Gordon Strachan is the most likely to step up to take it - and he rarely fluffs a chance to score. He believes in practice. "Part of training for someone who plays in an attacking role, is making sure your shots are on target from whatever angle - and that includes the penalty spot. I never like to rush to take penalites but to put the pressure on the goalkeeper."

DENIS WISE -
The Chelsea star proved several times last season that he can score under pressure from the spot-kick and he rarely tries the same style twice. "Goalkeepers learn quickly and can watch you on video. I try to vary penalties as much as possible,"

PETER NDLOVU -
Coventry's Zimbabwe international never gets flustered taking penalties. "If the penalty is a very important once I try not to let it get to me. It is better for me, if I can take it straight away. I practice my penalties in training."

TEDDY SHERINGHAM -
The Tottenham and England striker is nobody's fool when it comes to taking penalties. It's a case of Ready, Teddy, Go! When the referee blows his whistle, Sheringham doesn't hesitate. He knows immediately how he is going to take the penalty and doesn't like to give the goalkeeper time to think. And he's equally happy placing - or smashing the ball home. "I like to keep 'em guessing," he says.

MATTHEW LE TISSIER -
The Southampton and England star is an artiste with the ball and it is very difficult for goalkeepers to stop one of his spot-kicks. He is so unpredictable. "Most goalkeepers try to guess what you are going to do," says Matt. "I like to help them guess - and then do something else. A goal is a goal and just as important whether it is from yards out of the area at an angle or from a penalty."

P·E·N·A·L·T·Y
KINGS

TOMMY COYNE - the Motherwell striker specialises in outwitting opposing goalkeepers. He is very effective from just about anywhere in the box and deadly from the penalty spot. "I try to send the goalkeeper the wrong way if I can, then you are bound to score if you are on target. Sometimes I like to blast it but not very often. If you are concentrating on getting power into your shot you sometimes lose something in the accuracy. That's why I prefer to place the ball if I can."

IAN WRIGHT - the Arsenal and England sharpshooter doesn't need penalties to boost his goal tally, but he likes to take them anyway because of the challenge, the one-on-one battle of wits between himself and the goalkeeper. "You have to keep your cool when you are taking a penalty. You have to forget about the score, about how much the goal might matter. You just have to concentrate on sticking it in the back of the net. You only feel the pressure if you let yourself," says Ian.

JULIAN DICKS - Liverpool's former Hammer seems to have found himself an extra job by taking the penalties for The Reds. "You don't often get a second chance from the penalty spot, so you have to give it your best shot," says Dicks. "Personally I like to thump it so that it will go through the 'keeper if he happens to get in the way. As long as you have confidence that you will hit the net with your strike, it will take a great save to keep out a blaster," adds the Anfield defender.

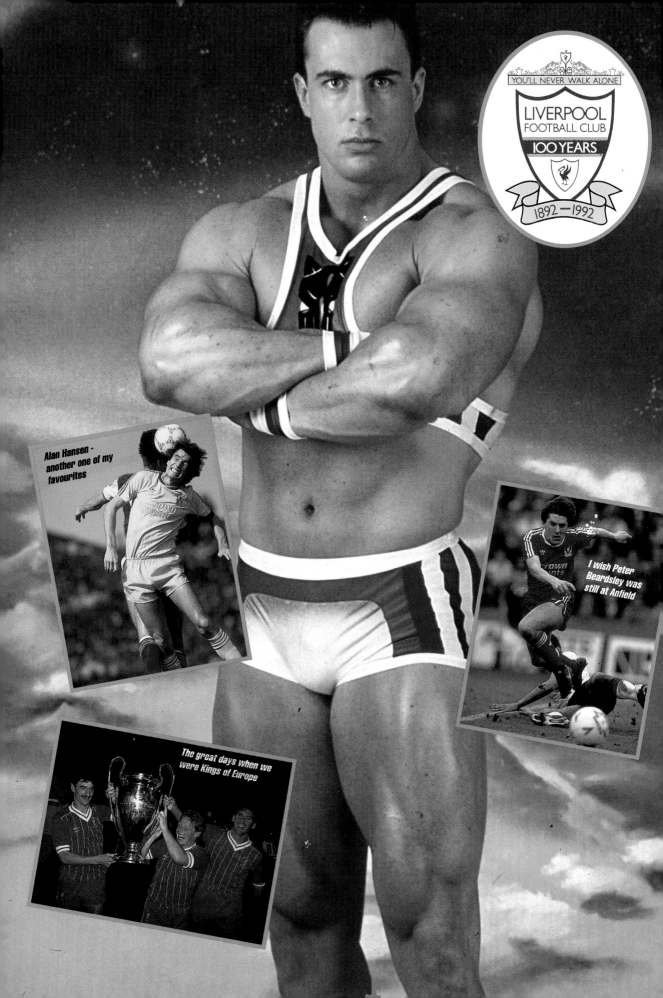

YOU'LL NEVER WALK ALONE

LIVERPOOL
FOOTBALL CLUB

100 YEARS

1892 — 1992

Alan Hansen - another one of my favourites

I wish Peter Beardsley was still at Anfield

The great days when we were Kings of Europe

Crazy

There are some people you would readily argue with about football and there are some you don't - one of those is Trojan from TV's megahit Gladiators. Mark Griffin is his real name and he is a Liverpool fanatic.

Although he was born in Basingstoke, Trojan has been a Liverpool fan for as long as he can remember and even fancied a career as a professional footballer.

"I used to play for my school and I dreamed that I would make it as a professional. In the end I knew I wasn't going to be good enough and I started a career in squash. It was only when I was injured when I was still in my teens that I started to weight train and that led to me taking up fitness as a profession.

"I qualified as a fitness instructor and also studied and passed in leisure business. It is a trade that I can always fall back on but at the moment being a Gladiator is keeping me very busy and I am getting more and more involved in showbusiness.

"I shall be in panto again this Christmas at Bournemouth so if anyone is coming to see it give us a wave."

But how does a lad from Basingstoke come to support Liverpool?

"It really started when I was at school. My mates mostly supported the London clubs. Many of them followed Chelsea. There were also Manchester United fans and even a few Bournemouth fans. I used to watch a lot of football on TV and Liverpool were on all the time. They never seemed to stop winning. I liked their style and before I knew it, I was a fan.

"For special treats I used to be able to go to Anfield now and then and also see them play in London. I still go to see them whenever I can get the chance.

"My favourite players in those days were Kevin Keegan, Ray Clemence and Steve Heighway. Later Alan Hansen, Kenny Dalglish came into the side and were brilliant. There have been many great names in the Liverpool shirt over the years.

"One of my all-time favourites has to be Peter Beardsley. He is still magic and I wish he was still at Anfield. I think that Ian Rush has also been great for Liverpool. He has been a fantastic goalscorer for many years. You won't find a better finisher in Britain.

"Bruce Grobbelaar is not only a terrific goalkeeper but great entertainment value as well. He was worth the price of a ticket on his own in his great days at the club.

"I know Liverpool have been going through a bit of a quiet spell by their standards but they have still kept a place among the top half-a-dozen clubs in the country and if they can do that when things are not so good, think what they can do when all the young players have that little bit more experience.

"There is a tremendous amount of talent at Anfield - Robbie Fowler, Steve McManaman, Jamie Redknapp, David James and Rob Jones are just some of the young players who have already made their mark and form the nucleus of a new generation at Liverpool I'm sure the Reds will be back at the top before very long."

Although Mark did not make it into professional soccer, he did fulfil one dream - he played at Anfield.

"I played in Steve Nicol's testimonial. It was an amazing thrill to run out of that famous tunnel and play in the stadium where I had only before been a spectator.

"If I had been a professional player I might never have got that chance. There was a big crowd and a great atmosphere. It was something I shall always remember, a fantastic experience."

Mark follows football in general even though Liverpool is his first love.

"I just enjoy the game. I have seen some great games at Anfield, especially against Everton but I will also go to see other teams..

"I'm not a Manchester United fan, but you have to admire them and their players, especially Ryan Giggs.

"I'm keen to see England do well in the 1996 European Championships. We must have our best ever chance of winning it. I really hope we don't blow it. We have the players, we have home advantage and I can't see us failing."

SNAPS

Somehow we don't think he'll get away with wearing these at Highbury!

'Do you know I'm really from Australia?' 'Nope, but you hum it and I'll play it!'

'I wonder if Mickey Mouse wears Vinnie Jones boxer shorts?'

Blimey, we know Everton had a bad season but surely he could have stayed in goal!

You need more than skill to be a star, you've got to be able to pull silly faces, too!

HOTS

'Not bad seats these for 10 quid, are they? Mind you, I don't think much of that kit!'

BOREDOM

'Did you hear the one about the Liverpool fan who thought he was funny...?!'

'I'm sorry Mr Ferguson, but do you think you could speak in English please?'

That's the first time Des Walker has got anything in the net for a few years!

Humble

It's every Premier club's worst nightmare - humiliation at the hands of one of the minnows in the FA Cup. Every year it happens and the heroics of the smaller clubs steal the headlines.

KIDDERMINSTER ventured into a place rarely seen by non-League sides when they travelled as far as the FA Cup Fifth Round last season. Their campaign began in October's fourth qualifying round when they beat Chesham 4-1 away in front of 1,144 people.

The prize was a home tie against arch rivals Kettering in the First Round proper. Harriers won 3-0 watched by 3,775. Woking were the next visitors and 4,411 turned up to see Harriers win 1-0 and earn a place among the big guns in the Third Round.

Neighbours Birmingham came out of the hat alongside them and 19,666 fans saw a sensational local derby in which the non-Leaguers dumped the First Division club 2-1 at St. Andrews.

When Preston visited Kidderminster in the Fourth Round they could not have been totally confident - and with good reason. They returned home empty-handed after losing 1-0 in front of 7,000 happy fans.

At last Kidderminster were rewarded with a home tie against a Premier side. They put up a great fight and were cheered off the pitch after frightening West Ham, who were relieved to go home with a 1-0 victory.

One of the most feared non-League sides is Yeovil who have the best giantkiller record of all. Last season they knocked Fulham out of the FA Cup and that made their 17th triumph over League opposition in the competition. They have also reached the Third Round 11 times, which is a record. Just look at some of their victims - Sunderland, C. Palace, Bournemouth (twice), Southend (twice), Walsall (twice), Exeter, Brighton, Bury, Brentford, Cambridge, Torquay and Hereford.

Now, is that Impressive or what!

DON'T mention giantkilling to Graeme Souness. He had nightmare after nightmare while he was the boss at **LIVERPOOL** and the last one helped him on his way out of the club. In recent seasons, Liverpool have been humbled by Peterborough and Bolton but they could not have expected to collapse yet again when they met Bristol City in last season's Third Round. The first meeting was abandoned at 1-1 when the floodlights failed. The rearranged game ended in the same score before City stole the show and walked off with a historic 1-0 win at Anfield. It marked the end of Souness' career at Liverpool.

Bristol City's Cup braves

heroes

Sutton's Matthew Hanlan helps to sink Coventry in '89

THERE have been some pretty sensational scorelines in recent years like in 1989 when non-League Sutton beat Coventry, who only two years before had won the FA Cup.

Coventry were the first to admit that if anything they were flattered by the scoreline which could have been more than 2-1.

There was the classic Cup-tie in 1992 when Wrexham beat a shocked Arsenal 2-1.

When non-League Woking beat West Brom 4-2 at The Hawthorns in 1991 a star was born as Woking's Tim Buzaglo hit a hat-trick. He was still being cheered as Albion boss Brian Talbot lost his job.

Among the other famous feats of giantkilling is the 3-2 win by lowly Colchester over mighty Leeds in 1971 and the 1972 humbling of Newcastle by then non-League Hereford.

Happy Harriers: Kidderminster's John Purdie and Neil Cartwright

WHAT DOES IT ALL MEAN?

"When we beat West Brom and I scored a hat-trick, my career reached a peak. I never wanted to be a full-time pro but all the attention from television and the newspapers and magazines made me feel like one. The actual game was over very quickly and I felt as if I was walking on clouds. It was almost indescribable - just fantastic."-

TIM BUZAGLO - Woking's 1991 hat-trick hero.

"When you come off after a defeat by a team that you should have had no problem with you feel dreadful. You want the ground to swallow you up. It is embarrassing, it is depressing, you feel very bad, your supporters feel bad and you know you are going to get it in the neck from your manager. It is also very frustrating because you relive the game and all the things that went wrong, but there's nothing you can do to change it."

BILLY BREMNER - Leeds captain in 1971.

"The FA Cup is all about little clubs meeting and beating big clubs - living off the dream of getting to Wembley against all the odds. It is like pursuing the impossible dream. I hope it never changes because the giantkilling feats are part and parcel of the unique magic of the FA Cup."

DENIS LAW - Ex Man United and Scotland

Eastern Promise

ASIAN soccer rarely earns much media attention in the West, but the game is definitely growing in that "corner" of the globe.

Some corner! Asia has getting on for half of the world's population, and the sheer weight of numbers indicates that their teams will improve as time goes on.

The game is comparatively new in the East, but the success of the Japanese experiment and the move to professionalism in China, plus occasional fleeting glimpses of other nations in the World Cup, all hint at late development turning into something really big.

National teams tend to be the focus of attention in most of the soccer-playing Asian countries - now over 40 strong. This is largely because the huge distances involved handicap clubs, who cannot find the money for regular travel and accommodation. National associations have much easier access to the finance involved.

Hence the success of the Asian Cup, begun in 1956 and now easily the biggest tournament on the continent, contested on the lines of the World Cup, every four years.

Only seven nations entered the first event, but now there is a lengthy qualifying process leading to a final tournament involving eight qualifiers plus hosts and holders. They play a league format in two groups, with the top two in each going on to knockout Semi-Fnals.

South Korea beat Israel to win the first two tournaments, by 2-1 in 1956 and 3-0 four years later. The Israelis made it third time lucky in 1964, beating India 2-0 in the final. Although they were helped by playing at home - six of the ten competitions have been won by the hosts - the Israelis were a fine team by Asian standards, inspired by striker Mordecai Spiegler.

He holds the Israeli record for games (79) and goals (24) and later had a spell with West Ham.

Iran won the next three tournaments, two of which were staged in their own country, and in 1980 they reached the Semi-Final before losing to Kuwait.

Kuwait then beat South Korea to take the title, and Iran defeated North Korea in the third-place match. So, over a period of four championships, Iran had won 15 games, drawn two and lost only one - a remarkable record.

The coach in their third success was Frank O'Farrell, formerly manager of Leicester and Manchester United.

Saudi Arabia then emerged as the dominant Asian nation, emulating Iran by reaching three successive finals. They beat China 2-0 in 1984, and in 1988 they scraped through on penalties against South Korea in Qatar, after a goalless draw.

Majed Abdullah, perhaps the finest Arabian footballer yet produced, was an outstanding figure during this period.

The 1992 tournament in Japan was the most successful Asian Cup so far. Crowds averaged nearly 20,000, with 50,000 to see the host nation beat the Saudis in the Fnal, staged in Hiroshima. Despite some unseemly violence, with eight players sent-off, the event was an attractive forerunner to the J-League, which began six months later.

Yes, football has certainly arrived in Asia.

Previous winners

1956
South Korea beat Israel 2-1 in Hong Kong
1960
South Korea beat Israel 3-0 in Seoul, South Korea
1964
Israel beat India 2-0 in Tel Aviv, Israel
1968
Iran beat Burma 3-1 in Tehran, Iran
1972
Iran beat South Korea 2-1 in Bangkok, Thailand
1976
Iran beat Kuwait 1-0 in Tehran, Iran
1980
Kuwait beat South Korea in Kuwait City
1984
Saudi Arabia beat China 2-0 in Singapore
1988
Saudi Arabia beat South Korea 4-3 on penalties in Doha, Qatar, after a 0-0 draw
1992
Japan beat Saudi Arabia 1-0 in Hiroshima, Japan

Japan - Asian Cup winners 92

PLAYING through the pain barrier is something that all our soccer stars will do at some stage if they really have to, but there are some who have had to endure more than most. We have chosen just a few players who have put their team before themselves. It's bravery beyond the call of duty.

DAVID SEAMAN

was in more trouble than Arsenal admitted when they were winning the European Cup Winners' Cup last May. To face Parma they needed every experienced player they could muster and suspensions and injuries had taken their toll, but England goalkeeper Seaman (right) was determined to be in the fray despite pain from a groin injury.

He needed three injections just before the game to take the pain away and he played through the pain barrier to keep a clean sheet and help his side lift the magnificent trophy.

DAVID BATTY

didn't want to miss Blackburn's last few games of the season so he was keen to play on despite breaking two bones in his foot. England star Batty did the damage playing against Aston Villa in early April and kept it a secret for some weeks as the race for the Championship between Rovers and Manchester United grew ever hotter.

"I didn't want to miss the run in, especially since we were neck and neck with United," he says. " I was quite prepared to have pain killing injections. When you get that close to the championship you will go through anything to see it through."

TERRY BUTCHER

was quite amazing in the heart of the England defence and showed just how brave he was when England faced Sweden in Stockholm needing a good result to qualify for the World Cup in Italy. Butcher (left) not only played the game of his life, but did so with a very severe head wound which needed many stitches. He refused to give up the game

Breaking The
Pain
Barrier

and played on with blood running down his face.

" You know you can get treatment as soon as the game is finished," he says. "When I start something I like to see it through. That's why I always stayed on the pitch if I could."

BRYAN ROBSON

was once described by former England boss Bobby Robson as 'a truly amazing player, the bravest, most committed, strongest I ever had.'

That is a fair description of Manchester United's former Captain Marvel. His catalogue of injuries meant that he broke, pulled, strained or dislocated just about everything possible but he always came back for more.

"You can't play football without getting hurt now and then," says Bryan. "You just have to not let it get on top of you. I don't mean that you have to be stupid and do yourself long-term damage but very often if you are totally committed to the game, you don't notice the injury so much until you stop."

There are acts of bravery every week, but perhaps the most famous of them all happened at Wembley in the 1956 FA Cup Final between Manchester City and Birmingham.

The City goalkeeper was **BERT TRAUTMANN,** previously a prisoner of war after being captured during days as a German paratrooper. He was very popular among English fans, but what happened during that Cup Final turned him into a legend.

He was involved in a collision with Birmingham's Peter Murphy, but played on in pain. It was only after he had collected his winner's medal that it was discovered that he had actually broken his neck!

"I didn't know much about it," says Trautmann. "I knew it hurt, but I was concentrating on the game so much that I ignored it until the match was over and we had won the Cup. That was so important to me. I was not a hero, I was just a crazy goalkeeper."

England captain Bryan Robson suffered a broken collar bone during the 1986 World Cup finals

Bert Trautmann broke his neck in this collision

Parrot talk

Throw back

It's a funny

MANY footballers have been called animals over the years and there have been incidents of dogs, cats and even chickens appearing on the pitch during a game, but there has been only one incident of a player deliberately taking his pet with him.
It happened back in 1899 when Portsmouth were in the Southern League, not long after they were founded. Their goalkeeper, whose name has been lost in the pages of history, was well-known as an animal lover and he used to take his pet parrot on to the pitch for the game. The parrot used to perch behind the goal. We bet the parrot got the blame if there was any swearing!

BEFORE new rules were brought in, there used to be a novel way of deciding who would have a throw in. Back in the 1870's if the ball went out of play there used to be a mad chase for the ball, Whoever reached it first would be awarded the throw in. Imagine that happening today, especially if the ball went into the crowd.

Cold blow bane

THE weather plays havoc with soccer nearly every season. Snow, torrential rain, highwinds, ice, fog - you name it, we get it. In 1987 Aston Villa's Charlie Athersmith actually played while holding an umbrella because of torrential rain. A team-mate borrowed a raincoat from a spectator, but the referee refused to abandon the game. Another ref did decide to call a halt to a match because of the freezing conditions. The trouble was that he was so cold, he couldn't blow his whistle and had to call one of the players over to blow it for him.

WHEN Aston Villa fans were travelling by tube to Wembley for the Coca-Cola Cup Final last season, a witty train guard had a laugh at their expense. "Don't be worried all you Villa fans who haven't been here for 17 years,"

Bright guard

he announced on the train's intercom. "The place has changed a lot since you were last here. But don't be embarrassed to ask for directions to the stadium, everyone will understand."
The Villa fans would like to have had the last laugh when their side beat Manchester United 3-1, but the guard had gone off duty!

Smokey Shearer

WHAT'S your favourite flavour of crisps? Blackburn and England striker Alan Shearer is well-known to like a plate of chicken and beans as his pre-match meal, but not so well-known is the fact that he is an addict of Smokey Bacon flavour crisps. He is so keen on them that his mates nicknamed him 'Smokey'. Good job his favourite wasn't cheese flavour!

Fool backs

AS they prepared for last season's FA Cup Final, Chelsea's heroes started suffering from back problems. Worried boss Glenn Hoddle sent for the doctor who said that many of them had sciatic nerve problems. That wasn't

very funny, but the reason for it raised a smile. The good doctor reckons that the players who were suffering spent too much time in their cars, especially stuck in traffic jams on the way to training. Glenn suggested that they might like to run or cycle to work, but the players said they preferred the back pains!

old game! game!

Black Arabs

IF you think that Hamilton Academical is a funny name, then take a look at some of the names that today's famous clubs used to be known by when they were in their early days. Arsenal began as Dial Square, Birmingham were first known as Small Heath Alliance, Carlisle were Shadowgate United, Oldham were Pine Villa, West Ham were Thames Ironworks, Coventry were Singers FC; Stockport were Heaton Norris Rovers, but perhaps the most novel of them all was the original name of Bristol Rovers, who were known as Black Arabs!

Dial-a joke

DERBY COUNTY'S American international John Harkes likes a good laugh. Not only does he play tricks on his team-mates, not only does he like to sing aloud and dance around the house on a matchday to get himself in the mood, but he likes to leave impersonations on his answer phone. When you call him you never know if you are going to hear John Wayne or John's cockney take-off.

Roger Milford - fan of Tina Turner , and Status Quo who hit the top of the charts with Manchester United last season

Sounds great!

THE roar of the crowd...the sound of the ball hitting the net. It's all music to the ears of our soccer stars. But there are other sounds they like - from rap to rock to reggae or from Motown to Mozart - they are all the favourites of the stars.

Sheffield Wednesday's Chris Bart-Williams is heavily into rap. He is rarely without his personal stereo and he even has a fair dose of it on his answerphone.

"I like different sorts of music, but I have always especially liked rap. I like the rhythm and I like the sound. I'm never far away from it.

Not many other Wednesday players like my kind of music. If I played it out loud on the team coach they would probably throw me off!"

The Beatles - still the best according to Liverpool ace Steve McManaman (right). Below: Phil Collins' music is popular with many players

Manchester United's Lee Sharpe will listen to almost anything, but he particularly goes for something a little on the heavy rock side.

"The first record I ever remember buying was 'Mull of Kintyre' by Paul McCartney and Wings. I have bought a lot of different things since then. I really do like listening to Meat Loaf. His brand of music really motivates. It gets you in the mood for a match," says Lee.

Talking about motivating, it is well known that Wimbledon play loud heavy rock in their dressing-room to give themselves a lift, but mostly to get on the nerves of the opposition. It wouldn't work with Nottingham Forest's Stuart Pearce - he loves it!

"I like my music to be really noisy," said Psycho. "I still like listening to the Stranglers and some of the old punk bands, but anything that is loud and answers to heavy rock will do for me."

A complete contrast is Aston Villa's Dalian Atkinson - he likes Spanish guitar music!

"I got into it when I was playing Spain with Real Sociedad. You hear it a lot on the radio, television and in the clubs and I really took to it. I bought loads of albums over there and when I came back to Britain to join Villa I brought them with me.

I have brought some more since then and now have a really big collection. I know some people think it is boring and I do like other music as well, but the sound of the Spanish guitar playing is really good."

Liverpool's Steve McManaman has the Mersey running through his veins and the Mersey beat in his heart. He loves all Mersey music, including the Beatles.

"I still like listening to the Beatles. They were totally different and their music still sounds fresh and good.

I still like bands like The Farm and Top. There is something special about music by the Mersey bands, they have something to offer that you don't get anywhere else. Shut me in a room with Beatles tapes and I will be quite happy."

Steve Bruce picks his music according to his mood. The Manchester United skipper has all kinds of music both at home and in his car.

"I suppose you could say that I'm an easy-listening fan. I will listen to classical music if I'm in that frame of mind, but I also enjoy

Motown, Sixties and Seventies music and a lot of today's sounds as well. I will listen to anything that is not too heavy. I like to be relaxed with my music, not be attacked by it."

It's not just the players who are keen on music. Referee Roger Milford is almost a fanatic.

"I like to have music in the car on the way to a match, it gets me in the right frame of mind for the game. My favourite is Tina Turner, but I'll also have a bit of Status Quo and various other things. I play a lot at home too, in fact, I am so keen on music I mix a lot of my own tapes."

A lot of players like to have a go at creating their own music. They'll play guitars, drums, keyboards, the saxophone - all sorts of things. Manchester United 'keeper Peter Schmeichel is a very good pianist, just like his father.

But perhaps the music champion of them all is England star Les Ferdinand, who has such a massive collection of CDs, tapes and records that you might think you had walked into a library instead of his home.

"I like music and I have a huge collection at home and in my car. The first thing I do when I get home after training is to put the stereo on. I've got hundreds of CDs and tapes. My favourite music is soul. I like Anita Baker and stuff like that. My favourite band are The Whispers. Great stuff."

Soccer ShoCKeRS

Invincible Preston

BACK in 1888-89, Preston's goal seemed to have an invisible wall in front of it. They conceded only 15 goals in the whole season and did not lose a game. Needless to say that Preston were easy Champions!

Mad Hatters

SPARE a thought for goalkeeper Willie Fraser. When he was at Sunderland he conceded 21 goals in three visits to Luton. In December 1958 he moved to Nottingham Forest and let in seven goals on his debut - then in his second game for Forest he played away to Luton and let in five more! Willie was born in Australia of Scottish parents which explains everything - he could catch the high balls, but couldn't get those down under!

Aldo's TV licking

HAVE you ever wondered what goes on while players are being interviewed by television just after a game. All you see on the screen is the head and shoulders of the player while he is talking, but sometimes they are only half-dressed or their mates are winding them up as they speak. One of the most bizarre was when Tranmere's John Aldridge (left) was being interviewed live on TV after playing for the Republic of Ireland - his captain Andy Townsend was on his hands and knees licking Aldo's big toe! Not many people know that!

Real Amazing

REAL MADRID set an amazing record at their fantastic Bernabeu stadium when they went from February 1957 to March 1965 without losing a home match. During that time they were held to a draw eight times and won the other 114 senior games.

Multi Sport Champ

ALAN HANSEN (right) is probably the most popular of TV's so-called expert commentators. Alan has a wealth of experience in soccer having starred with Liverpool and Scotland. But not many people realise he was also a youth international at both golf and volleyball.

Knock on Wood

HAVE you ever had one of those days? On October 4th, 1913 Norman Wood was playing up front for Stockport against Fulham in an old Division Two game. In the tenth minute in attempting to head clear from a corner he put the ball in his own net. Five minutes later he handled in his own area and Fulham were given a penalty from which they scored.

A little later, Stockport were awarded a penalty and Wood had the chance to make up for his mistakes. Instead he half-hit the ball straight at the goalkeeper who easily caught it.

There were no substitutes in those days otherwise Norman would probably have run off the pitch without being asked.

Boro Casualties

SOCCER can get a bit rough sometimes, but it's nothing new. When Middlesbrough played their first ever FA Cup-tie in 1883 against Staveley they lost 5-1 and every Boro player had to go to hospital after the game!

Villa Reject

MANCHESTER UNITED and Scotland star Brian McClair (below) is well-known to be a bit of an egg-head. He is one of the most educated players in the game, but few know that he joined Aston Villa as a 16-year-old and was later rejected. He became a Chemistry student and was still at Glasgow University when he gained a reputation as a teenage starlet after hitting a hat-trick for Motherwell in a 3-0 win over Rangers.

Fiery Albert

ANYONE signing Albert Nightingale back in the 1950's was taking a bit of a risk. He made 346 League appearances and scored 87 goals. That's not bad, so what's the problem? When he was at Huddersfield in 1951 their stand was destroyed by fire. In September 1956 when he was with Leeds, their stand went up in smoke, too! Good job he wasn't a striker!!!!!

Four goal loser

LUTON TOWN striker Kerry Dixon once scored four goals in a match on September 25th, 1982 and lost! He was playing for Reading away to Doncaster and the scores went like this - 1-0;1-1; 2-1; 3-1; 3-2; 4-2; 4-3; 5-3; (at half-time); 5-4; 6-4, 6-5, 7-5. That's where the game ended with Dixon (pictured) having hit four goals and he still finished on the losing side.

Smoking ban

PLYMOUTH ARGYLE manager Peter Shilton (left) is a fitness fanatic which is just as well because he is following quite a tradition at Argyle. Back in 1903 the club introduced a rule that players were not allowed to smoke up to four hours before a game. If they did and were caught they would be fined one shilling, or five pence as we now know.

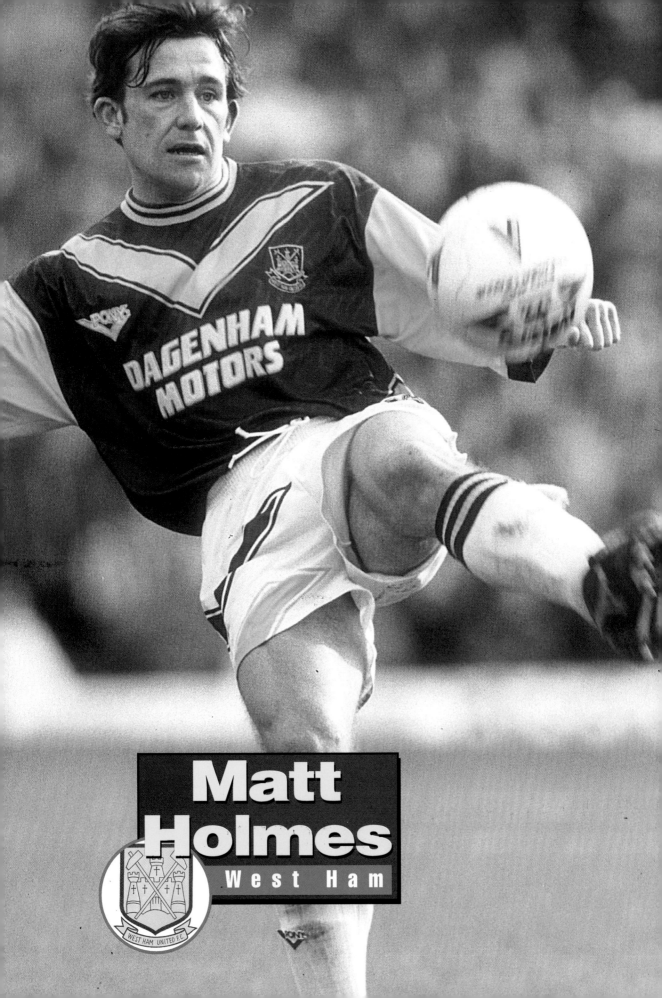

Matt
Holmes
West Ham

Rob Newman

Norwich

How **YOU** can bec

DO you want to be a top soccer star? How are you going to do it? That's the difficult bit, isn't it. Well, to help you, we've enlisted the help of super striker **TONY COTTEE** who has reached the top after first kicking a ball when he was just a baby. Tony tells you how he did it in ten steps to stardom.

STEP ONE

I was encouraged to kick a ball as soon as I could walk, but that doesn't mean that if you didn't you won't make it. I was just an early starter. My dad encouraged me a lot. The lesson is it is never too early to start practising your skills. Getting used to having a ball at your feet is the first step.

STEP TWO

Unlike a lot of people I believe that getting match experience when you are young does help. I played for a local Essex side, Romford Royals, in an Under-8s competition and it gave me a chance to get used to a match situation. Getting a proper game is probably the next step.

STEP THREE

If you are able to get into your school team that is really the next step. I used to play for my school on Saturday mornings and a club side on Sunday mornings. I was never one of those lads who played morning and afternoon Saturday and Sunday. I believe you can overdo it.

STEP FOUR

If you do well in your school's side there's a good chance you will be picked to play for your district. Your district side will help you get selected to play for your county and that's where the professional scouts will often come to see you.

STEP FIVE

When the scouts came to see games in which I was playing, I was given the chance to become an associated schoolboy with either Arsenal, Crystal Palace or West Ham. As an A.S. you go for training a couple of evenings a week and they watch your progress. I came from a staunch West Ham family

me a soccerstar!

the reserves and then, hopefully, comes that very special day when you get your first team chance. Everyone remembers their senior debut. It seems to pass very quickly but do your best to enjoy it - you might be back in the reserves tomorrow!

STEP EIGHT

Having made it to the first team, you want to make sure that you stay there. Don't get carried away and think you have made it. There is still a lot of work to be done - for the rest of your career! Keep your feet on the ground, keep your sleeves rolled up and continue to listen, learn and improve.

STEP NINE

If you do really well, you might get an international chance. Usually you will be given an opportunity in the Under-21 side before getting a call to the senior squad. In a sense it is like starting all over again. You will have a different boss, different coaches, different team-mates. Getting an England call is like the first day at a new school.

Hard work and practice made Tony an England star!

STEP TEN

You have won an England place, your family thinks the world of you - so that's it, right? Wrong! Never stop improving, never stop learning and never get complacent. You will hit patches of poor form and you will get injured and have to reclaim your place in the side. Step ten goes on throughout your career.

TONY'S TOP TIP

I cannot say enough about practising your skills. Hard work counts for a lot, but it is not enough on its own. The very top players are skilful players and they never stop practising or trying to get even better. If you want to climb to the top, practice the skills that will take you there.

---

so I didn't hesitate in joining The Hammers. Just before I left school I applied for work experience with West Ham and ended up training with the first team. I was only 15.

STEP SIX

If all goes well, when you are ready to leave school, the club will offer you an apprenticeship. You still have a long way to go so the thing to remember is that you must work hard, listen and learn and show that you really want to do your best. Having the right attitude goes a long way.

STEP SEVEN

As you progress you will get to play in

Do we want a Euro Super

IS a European Super League a dream, or could it become reality? The prospect of seeing Britain's top clubs regularly in League action against the best in Europe might be an exciting one for many, but for others it is a definite non-starter. We asked some of our top managers what they thought....

Top British clubs could find themselves playing against the likes of AC Milan and Parma every week

No! Ruin our game - Ron Atkinson

ASTON VILLA boss Ron Atkinson is no newcomer to European competitions. With Villa, Atletico Madrid and Manchester United he has sampled the high-profile and big match atmosphere of taking on the best of the rest.

The European spotlight suits a man like Big Ron. He has all the credentials to star as one of the top men in Europe and you might think he would welcome the chance - but you would be wrong.

"I think we have gone as far to a European League as we want to with the group matches in the European Cup." says the Villa boss.

"Playing in Europe is a wonderful experience for the players, the fans and the managers. But I would not like to see it become more regular than it is now.

"It would no longer be so special and I think it would mean so much upheaval on the domestic scene that it could ruin the very roots of our game.

"I am delighted that Villa re back in Europe this season. When you look at stars like Bosnich, Saunders, Staunton and the others in the side, they deserve the chance to show what they can do against the very best clubs but I think the knockout Cups are all we need to achieve that. I'm not in favour of more than that."

Yes! Need two teams - Alex Ferguson

MANCHESTER **U**NITED manager Alex Ferguson believes clubs would need two teams if they were to enter a European League.

"I can remember Walter Smith once talking about having such a large pool of players that it would not be a problem to pick one team for the European Cup and another for the Scottish Premier and I believe that that could be the way forward if we are compete in a season-long European Super League,"says Fergie.

"If not, it would be too much for the players - and possibly the fans, not to mention a very confused manager. I would be happy to give it a try but there would have to be changes at home."

League?

JOE JORDAN, who has played on the Continent as well as for Scotland, would love to manage a team playing in the European League.

"It is the highspot of a player's career to represent his country or his club against foreign opposition, especially in competition.

"I am in favour of anything that makes that possible just so long as commonsense prevails and clubs are not expected to take part in a full European League programme and a full domestic League programme, as well as all the Cup competitions.

"But personally I would like to see its introduction. It could be very exciting."

Yes! Cut Premier down to size - Trevor Francis

SHEFFIELD WEDNESDAY's Trevor Francis has close contact with Europe and would love his club to be more involved.

Yes! Rangers will be ready - Walter Smith

RANGERS manager Walter Smith is very keen on seeing his team challenging the best.

"European nights are always special and for us they mean a great deal. Perhaps when you are playing the same teams four times a season in the Premier and often meeting them again in the Scottish Cup and Scottish League Cup, Europe means that bit more, but it is certainly something we would be very interesting in playing in.

"We enjoyed playing in the European Cup mini-League and I can see that being a fore-runner of something much bigger. It can and will come, and Rangers will be ready for it when it does."

Yes! Play both - Kevin Keegan

NEWCASTLE BOSS Kevin Keegan has mixed views.

"I like British football and I don't think it should play second fiddle to a European League. But if it could be organised to play in both without killing off your players, then I'm all for it."

" The prospect of a European Super League is very exciting. The chance to pit your wits against the best of the Italians, Spaniards, Dutch, Belgians and so on, would be tremendous.

"The only reservation I have is that something would have to give on the home front. Perhaps if the Premier League was reduced to a dozen clubs who played each other twice and the other domestic Cup competitions were designed to accommodate the other commitments of the top clubs, then the European League would have a chance to succeed. It could be great."

THEY might be the smallest strike partnership in the business, but Chelsea goal pals Mark Stein and John Spencer are causing giant-sized problems for opposing defenders this season.

Spencer (5ft 7ins) and Stein (5ft 6ins) are living proof that size doesn't matter as they continue to rip teams to shreds and plunder goals galore in the current Chelsea revival.

Since coming together in an FA Cup Fourth Round replay at Sheffield Wednesday last season, the tiny terrors fired Chelsea clear of the Premiership relegation zone and all the way to Wembley.

Yet it's not so long ago that Spencer was ready to walk away from Stamford Bridge and look to rebuild his career in the lower divisions.

"When the boss signed Steiny for £1.5 million from Stoke, I thought the

Mark Stein and John Spencer...

Chelsea's pint

so far. Obviously it's meant a change in approach for me but the boss has made everyone in the team conscious of the need to get the ball to our feet.

"We're not going to bombard teams with the long ball, but that was never going to happen with Glenn in charge anyway. We've got to keep moving and keep passing."

Hoddle admits he didn't originally plan to team his pint-sized predators together but became more and more convinced his plan could work as he watched the dynamic duo in training.

"It was in my mind to pair Mark and John together a few weeks before I actually did because when we were facing teams who relied on set-pieces, we didn't have the power to live with them and had to come up with anyway way to counter them," Hoddle reveals.

"If we get the ball on the floor enough times to these two they will cause problems for any team in the country."

writing was on the wall for me and I'd have to move to another club to get first team football," admits the former Rangers striker.

"The way the English game is usually played, it's one big guy up front to win the high stuff and the little fella feeding off him. But we're proving that this way can work just as well.

"I always knew I could get goals in the first team but I wasn't sure whether I'd ever get a chance here. There was a lot of speculation about my future and the boss admitted that I was fourth in the queue behind Mark, Tony Cascarino and Neil Shipperley.

"But at no stage did I ever let my head drop because that's when you've lost the battle. I kept scoring goals in the reserves and now I've been given my chance in the first team I'm proving I can get goals at the highest level."

Stein struggled in his first few games for Chelsea after his big money move, but after seven games without a goal has hardly looked back since.

He admits he was surprised when player-manager Glenn Hoddle first teamed him up with Spencer and recalls: "It was a harsh decision when the boss left out Neil Shipperley, but he was only a teenager and there was a lot of pressure involved when a big club like Chelsea are struggling at the wrong end of the table.

"But John has come in and taken his chance really well. Some of his finishing has been unbelievable and with his scoring record he now tells the rest of the lads that I'm just milking the glory off his back!

"It was a brave decision by the boss to pair us together, but it's worked

sized predators

NOT all the big names in soccer play in the FA Premiership - there are more than a few stars playing in the Endsleigh Football League, too. SHOOT turns the spotlight on them for a change and gives the lowdown on six superstars outside the top flight

GARY McSWEGAN (Notts County):
It was a surprise when Rangers' starlet Gary McSwegen signed for Notts County in 1993 but he wanted regular first team football, something which the Ibrox club could only half-promise. It proved to be a dream move for both the 23-year-old forward and his club. He was one of the inspirations behind a team that only narrowly missed a place in the First Division play-offs. This season County are on a big promotion push and see Gary as an ace card, fast and effective. Only problem that County face is the usual one of keeping such talent for themselves. A return to Scotland might not be out of the question.

PAUL FURLONG (Watford):
One of the top strikers in the First Division - but for how long? The 25-year-old former van driver was playing for non-League Enfield when Terry Butcher plucked him from obscurity to join Coventry. He came into the side at the same time as Peter Ndlovu but after Butcher left, Furlong's career seemed to take a dive. Watford stepped in and he joined them during the summer of 1992. For the last two seasons he has been their top scorer and they'll be hoping that he makes it three in a row and help them to promotion. But, the big boys have been watching him and it could well be that Paul will be in the Premiership before long.

MIKE MILLIGAN (Oldham):
Back in the First Division after enduring relegation with Oldham, Mike Milligan will be at the heart of his side's battle to get straight back to the top flight. The Republic of Ireland international will be in his tenth season with Oldham during this campaign. It would have been ten already but for a sad season at Everton where things just did not work out. He was happy to return to Oldham in 1991. Now aged 27, the rugged midfielder led The Latics to the old Second Division Championship and a League Cup Final appearance in 1991 and he is keen to do it all again this season.

the best

STEVE PEARS (Middlesbrough):

Certainly one of the best goalkeepers outside the Premiership, Steve has often kept Middlesbrough's game alive by the sort of saves that you would normally expect to see in international soccer. It was a strange season for Boro last time round. At times they were battling relegation yet in the end they were only just pipped for a place in the Play-Offs. Their 32-year-old former Manchester United goalkeeper played a major part in their first bid for glory. Pears began his career as an apprentice at Old Trafford and originally joined Boro on loan in the 1983-84 season, making his senior debut with them. He returned to United for four games but in 1985 made a permanent move to Ayresome Park and has been No. 1 ever since.

STEVE BULL (Wolves):

The England striker has had eight years with Wolves and was one of those rare breed of players who got capped while playing outside the top division. An old-fashioned centre-forward, Steve made his England debut on May 27th, 1989 against Scotland at Hampden Park. Wolves had just won the old Third Division Championship with Bull hitting 37 goals. Steve came on as sub in the first-half and marked his debut with a second-half goal as England won 2-0. Despite injury problems he is still scoring goals.

ANDY WALKER (Bolton):

A cult hero at Bolton Wanderers, Scottish international Andy Walker was previously a hero at Motherwell and Celtic and even had a two-game loan spell with Newcastle during the 1991-92 season, just before he joined Bolton. The

29-year-old forward became a success overnight at Bolton, mostly because of his fantastic form and goals during the club's Cup giantkilling exploits. He was sidelined by injury for most of Bolton's important games last season but he is determined to help the side repeat their magical Cup form and grab a promotion place during this campaign.

Football's Famous Fans

FOOTBALL has always been the favourite game of the stars. It doesn't matter how rich, famous or successful you become, following your team stays in the blood.

Every club has its own celebrity supporter. Some are well-known for it - like former Government minister David Mellor, and Prime Minister John Major, both adore Chelsea. Others are just as loyal, but keep a lower profile.

Did you know for example that television star Bob Mortimer, famous for his comedy double act with Vic Reeves, is a lifelong Middlesbrough supporter? Or that singer Alison Moyet arranges her concert dates so she can watch Southend United as often as possible.

Madcap Mortimer is serious only about one thing - his beloved Boro'. "I'll having nothing said against them," he says.

"I first watched them at six-years-old. The only thing I can remember is being lifted over the turnstile. I think we've got a fabulous set of fans, certainly far better than the likes of Manchester United or Liverpool."

Showbiz folk appreciate the similarities between football and what they do for a living. Footballers have to entertain the crowd and are very much in the public eye. After actor

Tony Robinson has finished making people laugh as Baldrick in hit TV series Blackadder, he relaxes by going to Ashton Gate to watch Bristol City.

Small screen celebs who share Robinson's passion about the game include Eddie Large (Man City), Peter Cook (Torquay), John Alderton (Hull), Brian Glover (Barnsley), Warren Mitchell - best-known as Alf Garnett (Spurs) - and former EastEnder Leslie Grantham (West Ham) are regulars at their favourite ground.

Glover is so fanatical he takes a radio with him to work. During costume chances at a Saturday afternoon theatre show, he is likely to be found in the dressing-room, radio clasped to ear, to find out how Barnsley are doing.

The music business is closely linked to football through its superstars. Disc jockey David 'Kid' Jensen feels quilty if he misses a Crystal Palace home game, saying: "I suppose there are more important things in life than football but on a Saturday afternoon I can't think of any."

Take That star Robbie Williams is a Port Vale fanatic. When he mentioned it in an inteview, Vale suddenly got thousands of teenage girls interested in the club and sales of the club kit rocketed.

Politicians are used to having to put on a good display in the House of Commons. So they find it a pleasure to watch others have to perform under pressure.

Former Labour Party deputy leader Roy Hattersley is devoted to Sheffield Wednesday.

Overall, Chelsea are probably the club with the greatest tradition of famous fans.

Their glory team of the 1970s must have been the only side in history to receive regular trims from the world's most famous hairdresser, Vidal Sassoon.

Sassoon, still listens out for Chelsea's scores from his home in California, recalls: "Ive been a Chelsea fan since I was four or five.

"In the Sixties I remember Charlie Cooke, John Hollins and George Graham in the salon in Sloane Street for a pre-match shampoo, cut and blow dry.

"They were determined to look their best for the game. Too bad they lost!"

Grounds for OPTIMISM

How the fans will watch football in the future

THE DAYS of sitting out in the wind and rain watching your heroes on Saturday afternoons are well and truly numbered.

When the next generation of football fans take a trip to a game, they won't be going out for the afternoon, they'll be going in. Inside to indoor arenas that provide the ultimate comfort for spectators.

Sliding roofs, heated seats, individual radio and TV coverage will be the norm for supporters going to every stadium in the country according to the Sports Council's Chief Architect Geraint John.

"The way ahead for stadia is fans' comfort," he says. "In 15 years time they'll have warmed seats, be able to listen to commentaries and I can see them having a television on the arm of their seat for action replays and updates on other matches.

"I can also imagine restaurants and snack bars providing waiter service to your seat so fans don't have to miss any of the action."

Geraint says he believes the stadia of the next century will mean that going to the game will take up the entire day, with hours of entertainment being laid on for fans.

"I'm sure they will still have the big screen even though they will have a TV on every seat. It may well be that the screen is not used during the game but I can imagine films being show before kick-off," he says.

"The day will soon be here when you can go and watch the latest blockbuster movie before enjoying the match. They may even put on more than one match with a series of warm-ups to the main event."

Shopping malls and bowling alleys will also be incorporated in the 21st century grounds, which will cost around £150 million to build.

"There will be plenty to do outside the actual arena," Geraint says. "In the grandstands we will see shopping malls being built with shops open seven days a week to keep people coming to the grounds.

"And fitness suites which both players and the public can use will be around the ground somewhere along with a sports science clinic, a more advanced version of the sports injury clinics of today.

"To make sure there's no parking problems the majority of the car parking will be underground. The whole stadium will be self-contained."

Geraint believes pitches will still be natural grass in a quarter of a century and he says the playing surface is sure to be perfect all year round.

"Pitches will be watered automatically at the roots and fertilised automatically as well. All the groundsman will have to do is cut the

The Silverdome - America's indoor arena that Britain must follow

Bring on the grass!

grass! It will be that easy.

"Never again will you see the muddy goalmouths and worn centre circles that we see a few months into the season these days. If a part of the pitch does become worn, all they would do is bring on another pallet of grass and replace it.

"If these grounds are totally enclosed, the pitches will be grown elsewhere and brought in on pallets. That's what happened when England placed in the Pontiac Silverdome in Detroit last year - the playing surface should be perfect."

In the stadiums of the future, even the smaller grounds will be multi-purpose according to Geraint.

"Clubs will be able to cover the pitches to allow pop concerts to take place and I can see there being moveable grandstands to make the arenas bigger so that athletics can take place in them," he says.

"The technology exists now to do it and I think it will be a feature of the new stadia. The stands will be on hydraulic machinery - it already happens in America where stadia need to change shape for American football and baseball.

"Having stadia that can cater for different sized arenas means we would be able to host the Olympics and Commonwealth Games."

It all seems a long way from the cold tea and dodgy hot dogs that most fans endure at grounds today.

American grounds already have multi-purpose use

Man Utd's museum is a step forward

Giant X Word

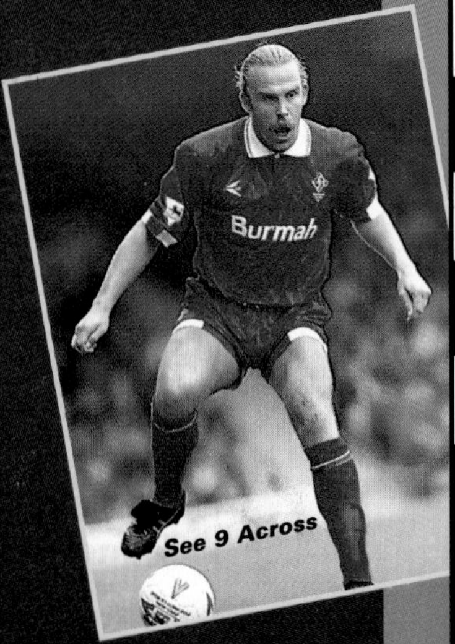

See 9 Across

See 5 Down

Crossword grid with partial answer "RAYCLEMENS" filled in across row 1, and "KKING" partially filled vertically.

ACROSS

1 South African-born 'keeper who became an Anfield legend (10)

8 Enjoyed a testimonial with West Ham last season and was then given a free transfer (4)

9 Former Coventry skipper who went on to play for Newcastle and Swindon (8)

10 England international who swapped Loftus Road for Hillsborough (6)

11 Wolves midfielder whose England career went downhill after he left Crystal Palace (6)

12 Something all fans will soon be forced to do (3)

13 An own goal could be described as this (4)

15 In short - Blackpool, Manchester City, Spurs, Liverpool and Crystal Palace have been on his ports of call (4)

17 Baseball Ground mascot (3)

19 Former Italian hard nut defender and World Cup performer (6)

21 See 3 down

23 Magnificent stadium in Brazil (8)

24 Type of transfer deal (4)

25 Roy and now Rocky have made this club famous (10)

DOWN

2 Second Division champions last season (7)

3 and 21 across Striker who joined Everton from Southend (5,6)

4 Gary at Wimbledon has made great strides this season (6)

5 Gangly defender who's played for both Liverpool and Everton (6)

6 To disallow a goal perhaps (4,3)

7 Saints defender Jeff (5)

14 A penalty could be awarded if the ball strikes this part of the body (7)

16 Brothers Rod, Ray and Danny (7)

17 Spanish World Cup star , Gordillo (6)

18 Former German international ace Felix (6)

20 Guided Forest back to the Premiership in his first seaso in charge at the City Ground (5)

22 Nickname of the Third Divison club from the Priestfield Stadium (5)

Answers on page 118

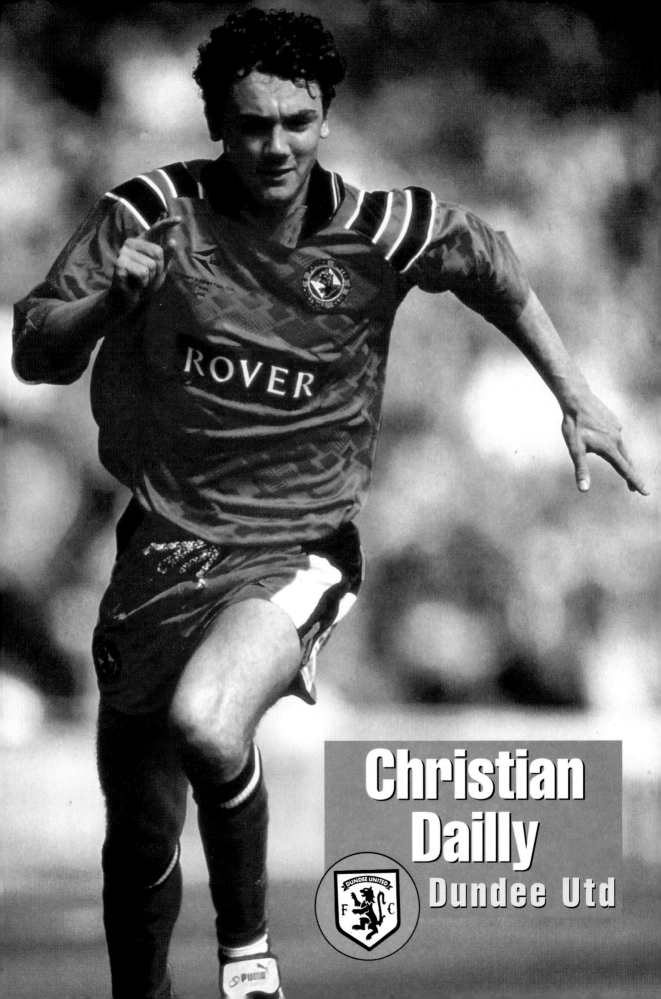

Christian Dailly

Dundee Utd

IAN
WRIGHT

WR

The Arsenal star leaves Everton's Neville Southall helpless with this blockbuster

Wright grabbed four
goals in England's 7-1
win in San Marino
in 1993

Close encounter as the
Gunner scores against
Wimbledon

GHT

WRIGHT

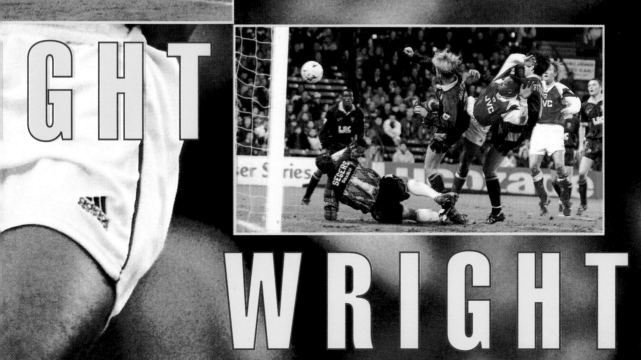

Carlton Palmer
Sheffield Wednesday

Mike Newell
Blackburn Rovers

From fan to fame for Geordie Gem Lee Clark

Local

Hero

Goalden

**Picture tribute to
First Division
Champions
Crystal Palace**

*John Salako - back to
his best after injury
nightmare*

*David Whyte scores
and Palace pick up
another three points
against Luton*

Eagles

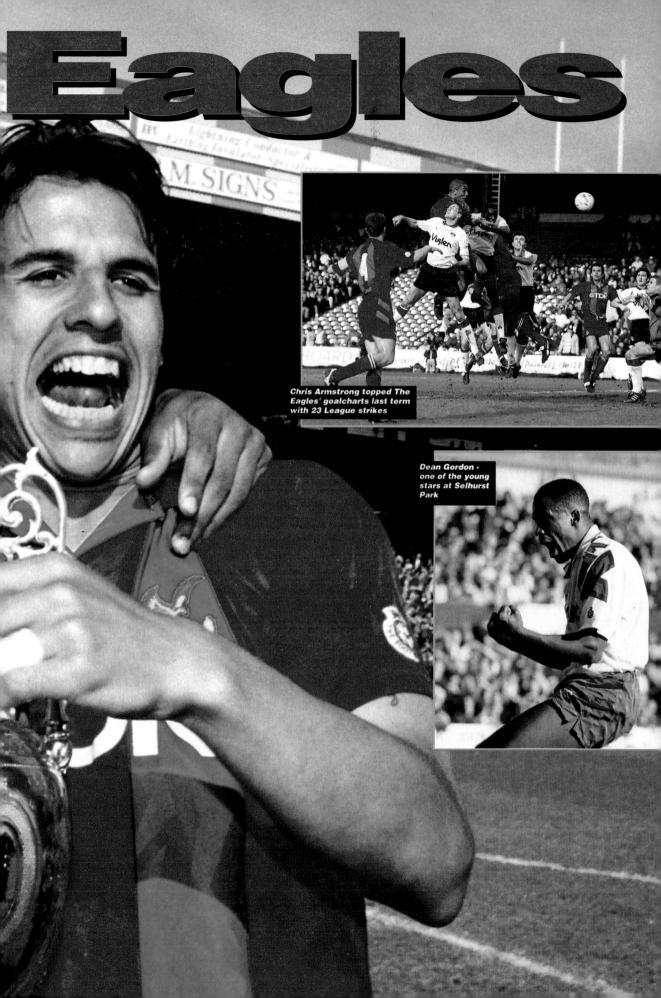

Chris Armstrong topped The Eagles' goalcharts last term with 23 League strikes

Dean Gordon - one of the young stars at Selhurst Park

Matt Finish: Le Tissier scores with this brilliant free-kick at Newcastle

Matt Le Tissier
Saints/England

The Saints star won his first England cap earlier this year

Europe

The Global Game

The

Americas

1. Which top award did Juventus' Roberto Baggio (right) win in 1993-94?

2. In which country do Neuchatel Xamax play League football?

3. Who finished runners-up to Bayern Munich in the Bundesliga last season?

4. From which Danish side did Manchester United sign Peter Schmeichel?

5. For which country is Anders Limpar an international?

6. Is it Thomas, Tommy or Tomas Brolin at Parma?

7. Which manager steered Barcelona to the 1994 European Cup Final?

8. Why were European Cup holders Marseille denied the chance to defend the trophy?

9. Name the three Dutchman who starred for AC Milan in the 1990?

10. For which country is Ipswich's Bontcho Guentchev capped?

11. In which country do Deportivo La Coruna play League football?

12. What country connection do Sheffield United's Jostein Flo and Oldham's Gunnar Halle have in common?

13. For which French club did Ray Wilkins and Ossie Ardiles play?

14. Enzo Scifo is the midfield playmaker for which of the 1994 World Cup contestants?

15. From which of the Moscow sides did Chelsea sign Dimitri Kharine?

1. How many goals did Diego Maradona score for Argentina in their 3-2 win over Germany in the 1986 World Cup?

2. Name the Brazilian striker who currently plays for Barcelona.

3. For which of the South American countries does Enzo Francescoli play?

4. Ipswich have two Canadian stars in their ranks. Can you name the pair?

5. How did United States international John Harkes make history in London in 1991 and then go on to reach new heights in 93?

6. Which number shirt did the great Pele wear for Brazil?

7. Name the South American country that was grouped with Germany in the 1994 World Cup?

8. Which Argentinian ace was banned from football for 15 months after failing a drugs test while playing for Roma in the 1992-93 season?

9. Is Mexican superstar Hugo Sanchez (left) a qualified dentist or vet?

10. He is famed for his frizzy hairstyle and colourful skills. Who is the Colombian star?

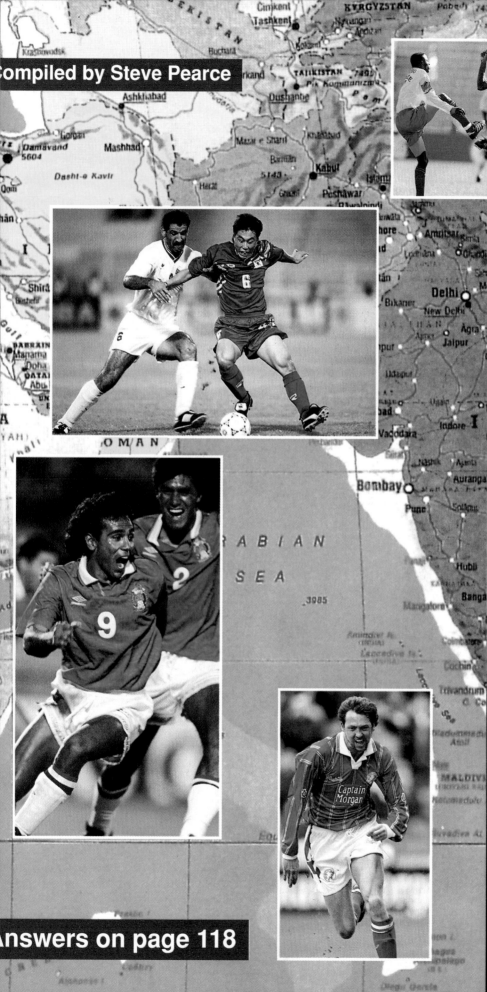

Africa

1. Which African nation produced one of the biggest shocks in world football when they beat Germany in the 1982 World Cup? Was it Algeria, Morocco or Cameroon?

2. And who also upset the big boys when they beat holders Argentina in the first game in Italia 90?

3. John Fashanu was said to be the target of which country, who were hoping he would play in last summer's World Cup?

4. But which Premier League star (above) did make his debut for the same country in 1994?

Australia

1. Name the Australian international (below) who has played League football for Swindon and Millwall?

2. Which country beat Australia in a play-off for 1994 World Cup qualification?

3. Which unique football boot did Australia-based former Liverpool star Craig Johnston invent?

Asia

1. Have South Korea (left) qualified for one, three or four World Cups?

2. Former Spurs boss Keith Burkinshaw has coached in this country, who qualified for their first World Cup in 1994. Who are they?

3. Which country conceded 11 goals in Italia 90 to their group rivals Germany, Yugoslavia and Colombia?

Answers on page 118

WINNERS 94

MAN UTD - Prem

ership & FA Cup

WINNERS94

ASTON VILLA Coca Cola Cup

WINNERS 94

RANGERS
Scottish
Premier
Champions

DUNDEE UTD
Scottish Cup

RANGERS
League Cup

WINNERS 94

ARSENAL
European Cup-Winners' Cup

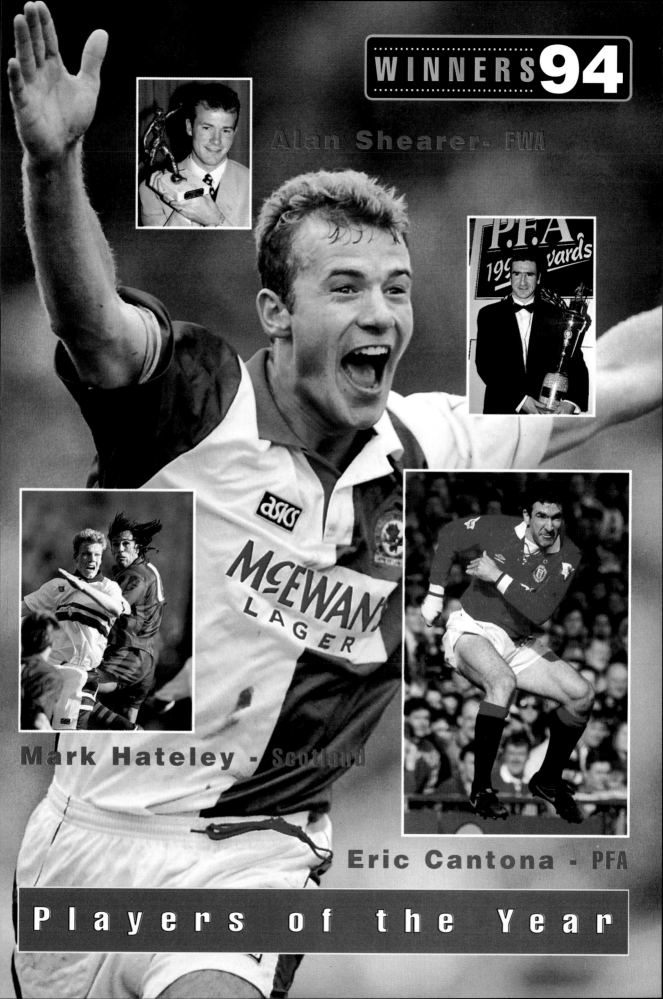

WINNERS **94**

Alan Shearer- FWA

Mark Hateley - Scotland

Eric Cantona - PFA

Players of the Year

Stuart Pearce
Nottingham Forest

Don't touch my SHOOT again

Make sure you get to grips with all that's happenin' in the game

Don't get shirty. Get SHOOT.

Britain's top selling soccer mag.

Question of Sport Answers

Picture Board: 1. Bryan Robson 2. David Hillier. 3. Mark Bosnich. 4. Stan Collymore. 5. Dennis Wise. 6. Ryan Giggs. Hone or Away: Home: Newcastle. Away: European Player of the Year. Mystery Guest: Dave Beasant. What happened next? Des Walker scored an own goal to give Tottenham the 1991 FA Cup. One minute round: 1. Howard Kendall. 2. Russia. 3. Ayresome Park. 4. Southend. 5. a) Lake. b) Woods. c) Swan.

Global Game Answers

Europe: 1. European Footballer of the Year. 2. Switzerland. 3. Kaiserslautern. 4. Brondby. 5. Sweden. 6. Tomas. 7. Johan Cruyff. 8. They were banned after being charged with bribery. 9. Van Basten, Gullit and Rijkaard. 10. Bulgaria. 11. Spain. 12. They play for Norway. 13. Paris St Germain. 14. Belgium. 15. CSKA Moscow. Americas: 1. None. 2. Romario. 3. Uruguay. 4. Craig Forrest and Frank Yallop. 5. He was the first American to play in a Cup Final at Wembley and the first to score there in the 83 Coca-Cola Cup Final. 6. 10. 7. Bolivia. 8. Claudio Caniggia. 9. Dentist. 10. Carlos Valderrama. Africa: 1. Algeria. 2. Cameroon. 3. Nigeria. 4. Efan Ekoku. 5. Zimbabwe. Australia: 1. Dave Mitchell. 2. Argentina. 3. Predator. Asia: 1. Four. 2. Saudi Arabia. 3. UAE.

Soccer Mastermind

Countries: 1. Australia. 2. Colombia. 3. France. 4. Uruguay. 5. Saudi Arabi, Bolivia, Nigeria. Players: 1. Neil Ruddock. 2. Tim Flowers. 3. John Fashanu. 4. Mark Hateley. 5. Peter Beardsley. Managers: 1. Ron Atkinson. 2. Graeme Souness. 3. David Webb. 4. Swindon, West Brom, Newcastle and Tottenham. 5. Stoke. Clubs: 1. Bayern Munich and Barcelona. 2. Hearts. 3. Bristol City. 4. Bury. 5. Man Utd, Oldham, Chelsea and Luton. Internationals: 1. Tomas Brolin. 2. Roger Nilsen. 3. Peter Ndlovu. 4. Jurgen Klinsmann. 5. Roberto Baggio.

X-word answers

Across: 1 Grobbelaar; 8 Gale; 9 Kilcline; 10 Sinton; 11 Thomas; 12 Sit; 13 Gaff; 15 Stew; 17 Ram; 19 Scirea; 21 Angell; 23 Maracana; 24 Loan; 25 Melchester.
Down: 2 Reading; 3 Brett; 4 Elkins; 5 Ablett; 6 Rule out; 7 Kenna; 14 Forearm; 16 Wallace; 17 Rafael; 18 Magath; 20 Clark; 22 Gills.

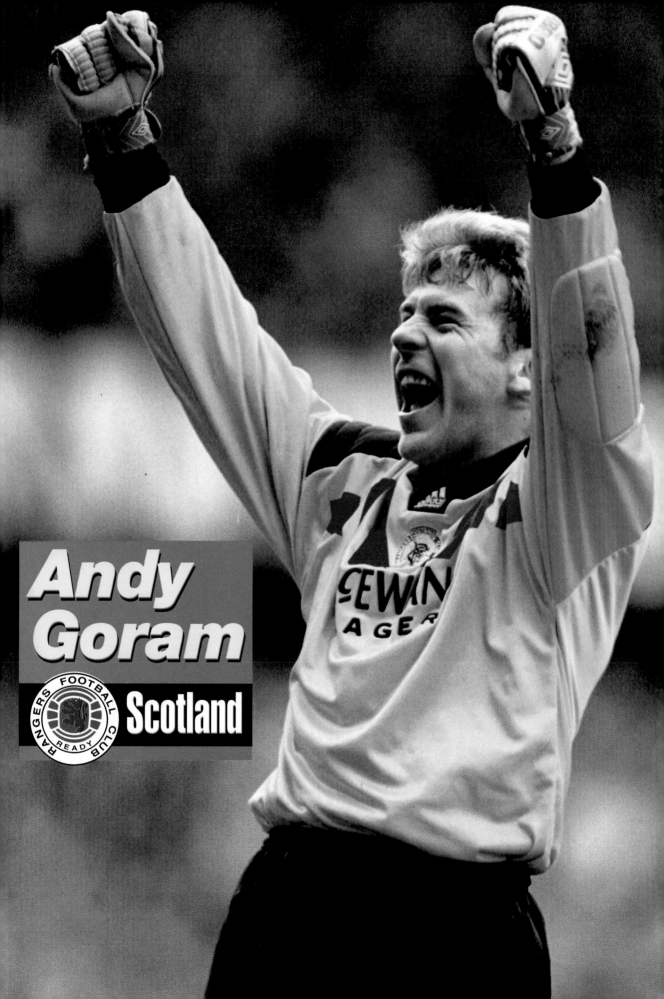

Andy
Goram

Scotland

WHO SAID THAT?

IT'S amazing the things you hear people say. Sometimes it is a commentator's blunder and sometimes a manager's excuse or one player talking about another. We have put together some of the best quotes of recent seasons...

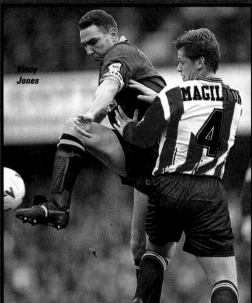

Vinny Jones

KEVIN KEEGAN, Newcastle United boss, after being asked what it's like to be a top soccer manager. *"You just sit there, pretend you know what you are doing and hope that you get it right."*

KENNY DALGLISH, commenting on Blackburn Rovers' chances in a match: *"We'll be trying to score more goals than them. If we achieve that, we'll win."*

MANCHESTER UNITED manager **Alex Ferguson** who missed out on signing Alan Shearer, but pulled off a masterstroke with **Eric Cantona.** *"If I had got Shearer I would not have been able to afford Cantona. It would have been much, much worse to missing working with a truly great player like Eric."*

GOALSCORING was a problem at **Everton** last season. One Goddison fan on local radio said: *"If* any of our players fell out of a boat, they still wouldn't hit the water."*

IF there is one thing likely to set a manager worrying about his future, it's being given a vote of confidence from the board of directors. Imagine how former Manchester City boss **Peter Reid** felt when he heard then chairman Peter Swales says: *"We hope Peter Reid will see this club through to the next century."*

TALKING of managers, **Dave Bassett** knows that his directors at Sheffield United do not tell lies, as he explained: *"When I accepted the job as manager of Sheffield United in January 1988, the chairman told me that I would have no money to spend. He has kept his word."*

MANAGERS don't just come under pressure from the directors, the players and the fans - they get it in the neck at home, too. Liverpool's **Roy Evans** explained; *"If my daughter Stacey had her way, Jamie*

Redknapp would be in the team every week, regardless of how he was playing."

STOCKPORT manager **Danny Bergera** said: *"I'd improve the game by completely altering the way we're brought up to play football in this country."* Nothing wrong with that except that Danny was born and brought up in Uruguay!

MISTAKEN identity can sometimes be forgiven in the heat and speed of the moment, but this one from ITV commentator **Brian Moore** took some beating. He was watching Leeds at the time: *"And now it's Dorigo bringing the ball away - no it's not - it's Rod Wallace."*

VINNY JONES searched long and hard at his ancestry to see if he qualified for Wales or even the Republic of Ireland. He refuses to believe he will never win an international cap and was delighted when Terry Venables was made the new England boss.*"I now think I stand every chance of making the England squad. Venners has seen the way I inspire the lads at Wimbledon and I know he's looking for a kit man."*

LEICESTER CITY forward Paul Kerr, when asked about team-mate **Julian Joachim**: *"When he learns how to*

run, he'll be frightening."

FA Supremo **Graham Kelly** has often been accused of being miserable, but he will have none of it, as he told us: *"When people really get to know me, they realise I have a great sense of humour. In fact, when people meet me for the first time, they are surprised. They think I am a short fat bloke, but I'm a tall, fat bloke."*

IT is trendy to practice your celebrations just in case you score a goal. Manchester United and England star **Lee Sharpe** has put in a lot of work on his:*"I'm working on an Elvis Presley routine which entails pulling up my collar, standing on the balls of my feet and using the corner flag as a microphone."*

We just had to include three classics from the past -

FORMER Liverpool manager **Bill Shankly** when asked about the UEFA Cup:
"I don't know anything about the UFFA Cup - we have never finished low enough to qualify for it."

FORMER Nottingham Forest boss **Brian Clough** at a Friday team talk:
"Now, who are we playing tomorrow?"

FORMER England manager Graham

Julian Jochim

Taylor, talking to a linesman when England played Holland in the match that virtually killed off England's World Cup hopes. The referee refused to red card Ronald Koeman after he had blatantly hauled down David Platt when he had a clear run on goal. Koeman later scored from a free-kick to secure a 2-0 victory for Holland. *"Tell the referee from me that he's cost me my job. You tell him that - from me. You tell him. He's cost me my job, that's what he's done. You just tell him linesman. You tell the referee that. Because he has cost me my job. And you can tell him that from me!"*

Jamie Redknapp

Born: 15.10.71 Nottingham
Height/weight: 5ft 10ins.11st 2lbs
Strengths: Has the incredible knack of always being in the right place at the right time. Full of confidence in his own ability and never afraid to shoot because most of his efforts end up in the back of the net. Enjoys an almost telepathic relationship with Peter Beardsley and is learning all the time from the old maestro. They have set Newcastle on fire.
Weaknesses: There were huge question marks against Cole's attitude when he was at Arsenal and that was the main reason George Graham let him go. Appears to have sorted himself out now, but occasional run-ins with Kevin Keegan suggest there are still a few doubts.
SHOOT RATING: 88

TERRY VENABLES–

KNEW HE WAS BORN LUCKY THE DAY HE WALKED INTO THE ENGLAND MANAGER'S JOB AND FOUND HIMSELF WITH MORE GOALSCORING TALENT THAN HE KNEW WHAT TO DO WITH. RARELY, IF EVER, HAS THE ENGLAND BOSS HAD SO MANY TOP QUALITY STRIKERS AT HIS DISPOSAL.

WITH THE EUROPEAN CHAMPIONSHIP FINALS COMING TO ENGLAND NEXT YEAR, UP TO 20 CLASSIC HIT-MEN WILL BE FIGHTING FOR PLACES IN EL TEL'S TEAM. SHOOT ASSESSES THE CLAIMS OF THE TOP TEN.

El Tel's

LES FERDINAND

Born: 18.12.66 Acton
Height/weight: 5ft 11ins. 13st 5lbs
Strengths: Superb target man who has developed the knack of 'hanging' in the air to win vital headers. Like so many of his international rivals, explosive pace is the key to Ferdinand's game. He has scared the life out of world class opponents in previous England games and has the confidence born out of that.
Weaknesses: Former England boss Graham Taylor hinted that Les needs to be feeling absolutely 100 per cent to deliver his best. If he is troubled by a slight injury doubt, he can convince himself he's not in the right shape to deliver his best.
SHOOT RATING: 87

DAVID HIRST

Born: 7.12.67 Barnsley
Height/weight: 5ft 11 ins. 13st 11b
Strengths: Strong as an ox and prepared to run through brick walls to beat a path to goal. His strength in the air and close control and turning ability means he can play either as a target man or the predator feeding off the big man.
Weaknesses: An horrendous injury record in the past couple of years has seriously hampered Hirst's progress and now it's questionable whether he'll ever recapture the form which once prompted a £4 million bid from Manchester United.
SHOOT RATING: 75

CHRIS ARMSTRONG

Born: 19.6.71 Newcastle
Height/weight: 6ft. 11 stone
Strengths: Fantastic pace allows him to run right through defences. Big, strong and powerful in the air, Armstrong is a fearless striker who never knows a lost cause. Manager Alan Smith feels he can be another Ian Wright and he has already turned down Nigeria to keep his England chances alive.
Weaknesses: Has yet to complete a full season in the top division and trails other England candidates in experience. His first touch is not always as good as it should be.
SHOOT RATING: 73

MATT LE TISSIER

Born: 14.10.68 Guernsey
Height/weight: 6ft 1ins. 12st10lbs
Strengths: The closest English football has to Eric Cantona, Le Tissier has fantastic talents and marvellous close control to help him trick his way through the meanest of defences. A dead ball specialist, too.
Weaknesses: There are still question marks against his appetite for battle and willingness to pull his weight when the chips are down. Spending so long at Southampton has also placed questions against his ambitions.
SHOOT RATING: 88

top 10 hit-men

continued over

El Tel's

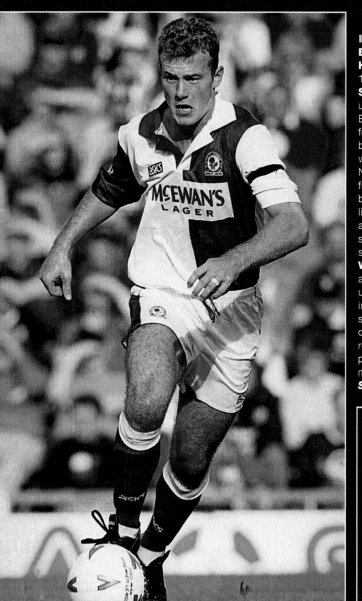

IAN WRIGHT
Born: 3.11.63 Woolwich
Height/weight: 5ft 9ins, 11st 8lbs
Strengths: The most unpredictable striker in Britain, Wright is a nightmare for defenders to mark because they never know what he is going to do next. Never afraid to try his luck from inside or outside the box, his explosive pace and lightning reflexes mean he is a constant threat. His scoring record at Arsenal speaks for itself.
Weaknesses: Ball control and self-control are not quite up to the mark for an international player and his scoring record for England doesn't make impressive reading. The only contender past his 30th birthday, maybe his time has gone.
SHOOT RATING; 90

ALAN SHEARER
Born: 13.8.70 Newcastle
Height/weight: 6ft, 11st 7lbs
Strengths: Speed, courage, strength, bags of confidence, lethal from short or close range, in the air and on the ground. Shearer has got the lot. On top of all that, he can also play with a partner or lead the line on his own in the 4-3-2-1 formation favoured by Terry Venables.
Weaknesses: The only criticism that can possibly be levelled at Shearer is that he hasn't set the international scene alight yet. But he will.
SHOOT RATING: 95

top 10 hit-men

CHRIS SUTTON

Born: 10.3.73 Nottingham
Height/weight: 6ft 3ins, 12st 3lbs
Strengths: Scores goals as well as he makes them, Sutton leads the line as well as anyone in his country and holds the ball up better than most. His height makes him an obvious threat in the air but has surprisingly good control for such a big man. Showed his class against continental opposition during Norwich's 1993 UEFA Cup run and has the added bonus of being able to play in central defence, too.
Weaknesses: Not the quickest player in the world and sometimes is too selfless for his own good, passing to a team-mate when he might be better trying a shot himself.
SHOOT RATING: 93

TEDDY SHERINGHAM

Born: 2.4.66 Highams Park
Height/weight: 6ft, 12st 6lbs
Strengths: Terrific aerial ability makes Sheringham an ideal target man, particularly if his Spurs team-mate Darren Anderton is playing to deliver the crosses from the wing. Signed by Venables for Spurs and successfully replaced Gary Lineker at club level. Now he believes he can do the same at international level.
Weaknesses: His first touch occasionally lets him down and though he is improving his game all the time, some might argue he is just a step short of international class.
SHOOT RATING: 86

DEAN HOLDSWORTH

Born: 8.11.68 London
Height/weight: 5ft 11ins. 11st 13 lbs
Strengths: An instinctive striker very much in the Jimmy Greaves mould, Holdsworth rarely takes more than three touches to put the ball into the net. Plays at his best with big John Fashanu as his minder but has no problems copying with the physical side of Wimbledon's game. Extremely confident in his own ability.
Weaknesses: Because Wimbledon's style is so unpopular with a lot of people, Holdsworth's international chances are always going to be hampered while he remains with the Dons. Not the greatest in the air and needs a big man alongside him.
SHOOT RATING. 77

SHOOT AN

Rangers won their
sixth succesive
League Championship
in Scotland

Published by
ipcmagazines
Distributed by IPC Marketforce
© 1994 IPC Magazines Ltd. England

Shoot! Annual 1995 is published by IPC Magazines Ltd., IPC Specialist Group 25th Floor, King's Reach Tower, Stamford Street, London SE1 9LS. Shoot! Annual must not be sold at more than the recommended selling price shown on page three. Sole agents for Australia and New Zealand: Gordon & Gotch Ltd. South Africa: Central News Agency. All rights reserved and reproduction without permission strictly forbidden. Printed in England by BPC Paulton books Ltd., Paulton, Bristol. Typesetting and origination by Meridian In Colour, Peterborough. Distributed by IPC Marketforce.